25

Ulysses S. Grant
Defender
of the Union

Ulysses S. Grant
Defender
of the Union

Earle Rice Jr.

MORGAN
REYNOLDS
Publishing, Inc.

620 South Elm Street, Suite 223
Greensboro, North Carolina 27406
http://www.morganreynolds.com

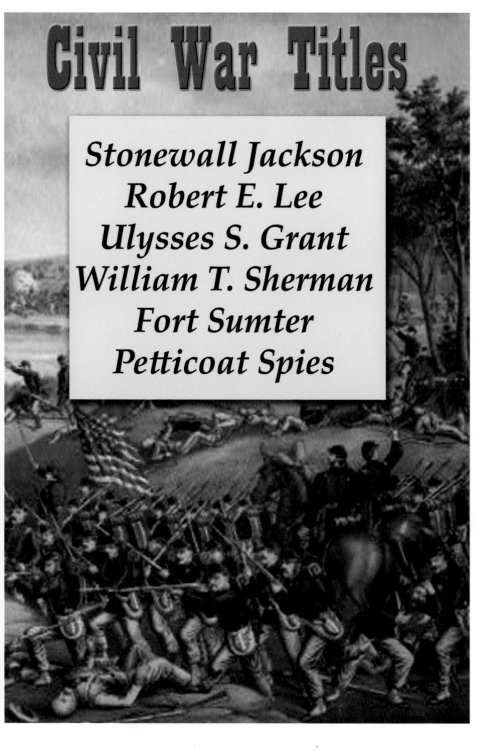

Civil War Titles

Stonewall Jackson
Robert E. Lee
Ulysses S. Grant
William T. Sherman
Fort Sumter
Petticoat Spies

ULYSSES S. GRANT: DEFENDER OF THE UNION

Copyright © 2005 by Earle Rice Jr.
All rights reserved.
This book, or parts thereof, may not be reproduced in any form
except by written consent of the publisher. For more information write:
Morgan Reynolds Publishing, Inc., 620 South Elm Street, Suite 223
Greensboro, North Carolina 27406 USA

Library of Congress Cataloging-in-Publication Data

Rice, Earle.
    Ulysses S. Grant : defender of the Union / Earle Rice, Jr.— 1st ed.
        p. cm. — (Civil War leaders)
    Includes bibliographical references (p.) and index.
    ISBN 1-931798-48-6 (lib. bdg.)
    1. Grant, Ulysses S. (Ulysses Simpson), 1822-1885—Juvenile literature. 2.
Generals—United States—Biography—Juvenile literature. 3. United States.
Army—Biography—Juvenile literature. 4. Presidents—United
States—Biography—Juvenile literature. I. Title. II. Series.
    E672.R49 2005
    973.8'2'092—dc22

                                    2004022345

Printed in the United States of America
First Edition

Contents

Ulysses S. Grant. *(National Portrait Gallery, Washington, D.C.)*

The Formative Years

When the man who became famous during the Civil War as Ulysses S. (U. S.) Grant was born on April 22, 1822, in Point Pleasant, Clermont County, Ohio, he had a different name. His parents, Jesse Root and Hannah Simpson Grant, named their firstborn Hiram Ulysses Grant and always referred to him as Ulysses, or simply Lyss. The name change came later, when the congressman who appointed him to West Point mistakenly changed his middle initial on an admission form. The new cadet could not correct the mistake. Years later, when the United States was on the brink of permanent splintering, some considered it to be an omen that the man who appeared to help save it had the initials of U. S.

Ulysses was born in the tranquil time in U. S. history that has come to be known as the "Era of Good Feelings."

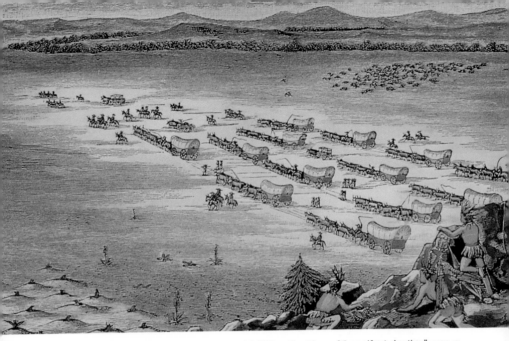

Heading west by wagon train and fulfilling the idea of "manifest destiny" was a popular choice for American families in the early nineteenth century.

Roughly from the end of the War of 1812 until the bitter presidential election of 1824, this was a period of national unity. The inherent conflict between the slave and free states was postponed by the Missouri Compromise of 1820. The focus was on expansion, and Grant's family participated in the westward movement. Beginning with Matthew Grant, the boy's paternal ancestor who landed in the Massachusetts Bay Colony in 1630, successive generations of Grants migrated south into Connecticut and Pennsylvania, and west into Kentucky and Ohio.

His father, Jesse Grant, a seventh-generation Grant in America, met Hannah Simpson in 1820, when he was twenty-seven and she was twenty-two. They married on June 24, 1821, and Ulysses, a big, strapping baby boy who weighed almost eleven pounds at birth, arrived ten months later. In christening him, the couple deferred to the wishes of the boy's maternal grandparents. Hannah's father favored Hiram; her mother, in a more romantic vein, opted for Ulysses because of her fondness for the exploits of the Grecian hero in François Fénelon's epic *Les Aventures de Télémaque.*

Ulysses grew up like most boys of middle-class background, living on the edge of the frontier. Jesse worked as a foreman in a tannery and a farmer until Ulysses was one year old, when he decided to move his family to Georgetown, Ohio, a few miles east of Point Pleasant. There, Jesse bought a farm, built a house, and opened his own tannery.

Jesse prospered in Georgetown, and the Grant family grew in concert with his success. Hannah, a hard-work-

The small house in Point Pleasant, Ohio, where Hiram Ulysses Grant was born. *(Library of Congress)*

Hannah and Jesse Grant.

ing, religiously devout frontier woman, gave birth to five more children over the next sixteen years: Samuel Simpson Grant (1825); Clara Rachel (1828); Virginia "Jennie" Paine (1832); Orvil Lynch (1835); and Mary Frances (1839). Jesse was outspoken and ambitious; apparently, Ulysses inherited his quiet reserve from his mother. "He was always a steady, serious sort of boy, who took everything in earnest," Hannah said of Ulysses in a later interview. "Even when he played he made a business of it."

In actuality, the demands of school and work left little

time for play during Lyss's formative years. According to Grant, most of his teachers were "incapable of teaching much, even if they imparted all they knew." Whatever the schools might have lacked in academic sophistication, they compensated for in the application of discipline. In this regard, John D. White, Grant's teacher at Georgetown, left young Lyss with an enduring recollection of how frontier teachers maintained order in the classroom: "I can see [him] now, with his long beech switch always in his hand. It was not always the same one, either. Switches were brought in bundles, from a beech wood near the school house, by the boys for whose benefit they were intended. Often a whole bundle would be used up in a single day."

While the discipline administered by Mr. White might have benefited Lyss later in life, it did little to spur his interest in schoolwork. He never stood out as a student in the one-room schoolhouse. Nor did he overachieve scholastically later during one-year stints at boarding schools in Maysville, Kentucky, and in Ripley, Ohio. "I was not studious in habit, and probably did not make progress enough to compensate for the outlay for board and tuition," Grant recalled later. "At all events, both winters were spent in going over the same old arithmetic and repeating: 'A noun is the name of a thing' . . . until I had come to believe it."

Ulysses learned to tolerate school but never grew to like it. He showed ability in mathematics but was rated about average in grammar, geography, and spelling. He particularly hated to speak before the classroom. Thomas Upham, who taught at Georgetown for two years, later remembered a time when Ulysses was called upon to recite Washington's Farewell Address: "[Ulysses] made fearful work of it, and after school said he would 'never speak there again, no matter what happened.'" His innate shyness would carry over into his adult years.

Outside the classroom, Grant developed a special affinity for horses. His parents allowed him to play in the stalls, under the bellies of the horses. Hannah ignored frequent warnings from neighbors that Lyss was endangered crawling among the feet of the horses or swinging on their tails. "Horses seem to understand Ulysses," his mother said. At about age seven or eight, he began driving a team of horses and hauling all the wood used in his family's house and shops. Jesse doubted that his son could "hold out for over a week—he was such a little bit of a fellow," so he hired a man to accompany him and to help out. A week later, the man told Jesse he was not needed because the boy "understands the team and can manage it as well as I can, and better, too!"

Farmers soon began to bring spirited colts to Jesse's tannery for Ulysses to train. Crowds of villagers often gathered to watch the boy put the unruly horses through their paces. He rarely raised his voice to the animals, preferring to win their confidence with gentle firmness. In his quiet way, the boy formed a bond with even the most cantankerous animals and never met a horse that could throw him.

On one occasion, a neighbor named Ralston offered a fine-looking colt for sale for $25. Lyss wanted the colt more than anything and Jesse, after his son pleaded, finally relented and gave Lyss the money, along with some instructions on the art of horse-trading. The boy hurried off to buy the colt and—as Grant recounted later— blurted out to its owner: "Papa says I may offer you twenty dollars for the colt, but if you won't take that, I am to offer you twenty-two and a half, and if you won't take that, I am to give you twenty-five." Mr. Ralston willingly accepted the latter figure. When the village boys learned of Lyss's naive transaction, they took great amusement in reminding him about it for a long time.

When about eleven, Ulysses began working on his father's farm. He later wrote, "From that age until seventeen I did all the work done with horses; such as breaking up the land, furrowing, ploughing corn and potatoes, bringing in the crops when harvested, hauling all the wood, besides tending two or three horses, a cow or two, and sawing wood for the stoves, etc., while still attending school."

Lyss's work ethic and sense of responsibility were rewarded. "For this I was compensated," he noted later, "by the fact that there was never any scolding or punishing by my parents; no objections to rational enjoyments, such as fishing, going to the creek to swim in the summer, taking a horse and visiting my grandparents in the adjoining county, fifteen miles off." Lyss also learned to shoot and actually became a good marksman, but he drew the line at hunting. "He was unusually sensitive to pain," a friend recalled years later, "and his aversion to taking any form of life was so great that he would not hunt."

The year Lyss turned seventeen, his father came to him and announced, "I believe you are going to receive the appointment."

"What appointment?" Lyss asked.

"To West Point; I have applied for it."

Jesse had learned that a neighbor's son had been dismissed from the U.S. Military Academy at West Point, New York. Jesse figured an appointment to the academy represented an ideal way for Ulysses to earn a higher education at government expense. Without first consulting Ulysses, he had submitted his son's name as a replacement to fill the vacancy. Ulysses felt little urge to become a soldier and did not aspire to a military career. "A military life had no charms for me," he noted years later, although he took pride in his country and family. His family, he often stated, had been American "for generations, in all its branches, direct and collateral." This esteem for country and family, which he acquired in his early years, would later motivate, comfort, and sustain him throughout his turbulent military and political careers.

Grant's appointment to West Point came on March 3, 1839, through the office of United States Representative Thomas Hamer, a friend of the family. Ulysses had little choice but to begin packing. Two months later, he

The U.S. Military Academy at West Point, as it was portrayed around the time Grant arrived there in the late 1830s. *(Library of Congress)*

boarded a steamboat at Ripley for the trip to the U.S. Military Academy.

The new plebe, as freshmen at the academy are known, carried with him a trunk full of belongings. Thumbtacks on the trunk's exterior spelled out his initials—H.U.G. Anticipating his initials would surely evoke derision from his classmates at West Point, the still-shy Grant— who stood just over five feet tall and weighed only 117 pounds—switched the tacks to read U.H.G.

This precaution, however, proved unnecessary. The Academy at West Point stands on a bluff overlooking a wide bend in the Hudson River, about fifty miles north of New York City. When Grant arrived at the end of May, he checked for his name on the roll of incoming cadets and found only a "Ulysses S. Grant" listed. Upon investigation he learned that his sponsor, Congressman Hamer, had incorrectly entered his first name as Ulysses on the application, adding S as a middle initial in the mistaken belief that it stood for Hannah's maiden name. By this slip of a pen, a new American legend began to take shape.

Grant's classmates pounced on his initials. One remarked that the "U. S." must stand for "United States." William Tecumseh Sherman, an upperclassman from Ohio, said, "No, it stands for "Uncle Sam.'" The impromptu nickname stuck. Everyone who attended West Point while Grant was there would always know him as Sam Grant.

When Grant entered the Academy, the corps of cadets numbered 250. They were divided into four classes in descending order: first, second, third, and fourth (plebe). The select roster of officers-in-training during Grant's four years at the Point contained several names destined for future military fame. William T. Sherman and George H. Thomas both graduated in 1840. One would eventually become Grant's good friend and the other one of his chief rivals.

Sherman, the wit of his class, was intelligent, aggressive, and imaginative, with all the qualities essential to the consummate soldier. His destiny awaited him in Georgia where his concept of "total war" would reward him with equal amounts of fame and reproach. By contrast, the less exuberant George Thomas—nicknamed

"George Washington" by his classmates because of his imposing stature—was grave of nature and a virtual "rock" of determination, which he would later demonstrate as a Union general at the battle of Chickamauga.

Other notable figures Grant came to know at West Point—some better than others—included the caustic Richard S. Ewell and the backward but resolute Thomas J. Jackson of Virginia (later known as "Stonewall"); the tentative William S. Rosecrans of Ohio; the energetic Winfield Scott Hancock and the intellectual George B. McClellan of Pennsylvania; Earl Van Dorn, a fiery maverick from Mississippi; the arrogant John Pope and the altruistic Simon Bolivar Buckner of Kentucky. Of all Grant's acquaintances at the Academy, however, it was James "Pete" Longstreet of Georgia with whom he developed his fondest friendship.

Grant and Longstreet made a curious pair. Longstreet, a hulking figure of a man, towered over his diminutive friend. He was one of the largest men ever to attend West Point—as well as one of the most rambunctious. Pete, as he was called, enjoyed contact sports, bayonet drill, swordsmanship, and military exercises. He considered Sam Grant of "delicate frame" and too "fragile" to compete in sports. In an interview years later, Longstreet assessed his friend's chief characteristics as "a girlish modesty; a hesitancy in presenting his own claims; a taciturnity [self-restraint] born of his modesty; but a thoroughness in the accomplishment of whatever task was assigned to him. We became fast friends at our first meeting." Longstreet further described Grant as having "a noble, generous heart, a loveable character, and a sense of honor which was so perfect . . . that in numerous cabals [groups of secret intriguers] which were often formed his name was never mentioned."

Another classmate described Grant as small but muscular and active. "His hair was reddish brown and his eyes grey-blue," the cadet recalled. "We all liked him. He had no bad habits." As small and good-natured as he was, however, Grant had a low tolerance for bullies, as classmate Jack Lindsey found out early in their West Point tenures.

One day while the cadets lined up at the mess hall, Lindsey, the tall, solidly built son of an Army colonel, shoved Grant out of line and took his place. Grant warned the much larger Lindsey against doing it again. The next time the cadets lined up at the hall, Lindsey did it again. Grant immediately plowed into him, knocked him flat and, with fists made rockhard from a decade of working with horses, delivered a punishment sufficient to discourage future line breaking. Word of Grant's actions rippled throughout the cadet corps. No one again attempted to bully him.

Grant later stated that, at the time, he still "had not the faintest idea of staying in the army," even if he graduated, which he doubted he would. Nevertheless, he adapted quickly to the drilling, hazing, and the ongoing need to respond instantly and unquestioningly to the often harassing commands of the upperclassmen, or to the resonant tattoos of a bugle's blare.

The curriculum was designed to produce officers and gentlemen. Mathematics, physics (or "philosophy" as it was known then), and engineering were the cornerstones of the curriculum that supported a wide variety of peripheral subjects, from infantry tactics to drawing. Grant settled in at about the middle of his class academically and stayed there for his entire four years at the academy. He did well in mathematics and even entertained hopes of someday becoming a mathematics professor. He fared less well in science, did poorly in French, and earned a few demerits (marks for poor behavior, classroom errors, or other violations). Grant later conceded: "I did not take hold of my studies with avidity, in fact I rarely read over a lesson the second time during my entire cadetship." He did, however, take advantage of the academy's library to acquaint himself with the literary works of Edward Bulwer-Lytton, James Fenimore Cooper, Frederick Marryat, Sir Walter Scott, Washington Irving, Charles Lever, and others. In sports, despite his small size, he performed well as a speedy rightwinger in rugby, and, not surprisingly, he excelled in horsemanship.

One of Grant's most memorable moments at West Point came when the imposing General Winfield Scott, the army's general in chief, visited the academy and reviewed the cadets. Nicknamed "Old Fuss and Feathers" because of his strict adherence to the finer points of military decorum and formality, Scott's "colossal size and showy uniform" captured Grant's imagination. To

General Winfield Scott reviewing his troops with the ceremony and pomp that gave him the nickname "Old Fuss and Feathers." *(Library of Congress)*

the diminutive cadet, the general was "the finest specimen of manhood my eyes had ever beheld, and the most to be envied." Grant secretly wished for the day when he himself would stand in the general's place on review. But as Grant put it: "My experience in a horse-trade ten years before, and the ridicule it caused me, were too fresh in my mind for me to communicate this presentiment to even my most intimate chum."

Perhaps Grant's proudest moment at the academy came just before graduation when his riding instructor called upon him for a demonstration in front of the entire corps. Aboard a powerfully built chestnut-sorrel horse named York—a horse that only two cadets could ride and that only Grant could ride well—he thundered toward a jumping bar set higher than the instructor's head. An onlooking plebe recalled: "The horse increased his pace, and measured his strides for the great leap before him, bounded into the air, and cleared the bar, carrying his rider as if man and beast were welded together. The spectators were breathless." Grant and his steed set a jumping record that day that stood for twenty-five years.

Grant graduated the next day, finishing twenty-first in a class of thirty-nine (out of an original enrollment of sixty-three), and was commissioned a brevet (temporary) second lieutenant. In the three subjects that counted most—mathematics, physics, and engineering—he ranked in the top third of the West Point class of 1843. Those at the top were assigned to the engineers; the rest were sent to the combat branches. Grant, again not surprisingly, asked for a cavalry assignment (a division on horseback) but there were no vacancies at the time. His second choice—the 4th Infantry at Jefferson Barracks, just outside St. Louis, Missouri—was approved.

West Point graduates were granted three months of leave before reporting to their new duty stations. Be-

Grant, his stature somewhat dwarfed by his epaulets, is pictured here in uniform just after his graduation from West Point.

cause uniform styles varied among the army branches, Grant had to wait for confirmation of his duty assignment before ordering his tailored infantry uniform. It arrived when he was home on leave in Ohio. His folks by then had moved to Bethel, ten miles from Georgetown. He tried it on at once. "I was impatient to see how it looked," he recalled later, "and probably wanted my old school-mates, particularly the girls, to see me in it." He still weighed 117 pounds, but he had grown several inches taller in four years. But even in an infantry lieutenant's uniform, he hardly presented an imposing figure, as he soon found out.

One day, he rode off to Cincinnati on a newly purchased horse, wearing his new uniform with his sword dangling at his side. He expected to become the object of awe and admiration but instead became the target of ridicule. A raggedly little boy watched Grant scornfully as he rode past, then hollered after him: "Soldier! Will you work? No siree—I'll sell my shirt first!" The boy's derision pained the new officer. A second incident later that evening also cut him deeply. Back in Bethel, he encountered a drunken stable hand who was parading up and down the street dressed in a makeshift imitation of Grant's uniform and evoking gales of laughter from the townsfolk.

Given the sources of Grant's embarrassment—a ragamuffin and a drunkard—he should not have taken either incident to heart, but he did. Between them, he wrote later, they "gave me a distaste for military uniform that I never recovered from." For the rest of his military career, Grant never again tried to dazzle anyone with his military regalia and never wore a sword unless he was ordered to do so. In manners of dress and conversation, he disdained ostentation and kept to the plain, the simple, and the functional.

On the last day of September 1843, Brevet Second Lieutenant Ulysses S. Grant reported for duty with the 4th Infantry at Jefferson Barracks. By then, West Point had left its mark on him. He discovered, to his surprise, that he was actually starting to like military life.

Love and War Games

Jefferson Barracks, America's principal bastion on the Western frontier and home of the U.S. 3rd and 4th Infantry Regiments, occupied a seventeen-hundred-acre reservation on the west bank of the Mississippi River, ten miles south of St. Louis. Colonel Stephen Watts Kearny, whom General Winfield Scott called "a perfect soldier," and "the bravest man I ever knew," was the commander. Kearny believed in reasonable discipline but shunned the overly picky variety exercised by many post commanders.

Grant liked Kearny's leadership style from the start. "It did seem to me, in my early army days, that too many of the older officers, when they came to command posts, made it a study to think what orders they could publish to annoy their subordinates and render them uncomfortable," he noted. By contrast, so long as Kearny's officers discharged their responsibilities properly while on duty, he allowed them some freedom in their off-duty hours. Grant took note of his new superior's even-handed approach to command.

General Stephen Watts Kearny.

The 4th Infantry, a regiment numbering twenty-one officers and 449 enlisted men, was divided into eight companies. Grant was assigned to I Company, where he would learn the trade of a company officer. Classmate Robert Hazlett reported to the regiment along with Grant. James Longstreet and Richard Ewell had arrived the year before. The officer corps was a small, select fraternity whose members often came to know each other. The family of Fred Dent, Grant's academy room-mate and Longstreet's cousin, lived only five miles from the garrison. Dent had been assigned to Fort Towson, in what was then called Indian Territory, but he had encouraged Grant and Longstreet to visit his home in his absence. Grant and Longstreet took advantage of the standing invitation often.

The earliest known photograph of White Haven, taken in 1860.

Dent's parents owned 925 acres of fertile Missouri bottomland. The Dents, who were originally from Maryland, named their estate White Haven after the family's tidewater holdings on the eastern seaboard. The father, Frederick F. Dent, went by the title of "Colonel." Although he had never served in the military, his self-appointed title was one commonly adopted by southern landowners. The elder Dent was large of frame and had a quarrelsome, contrary nature. A local doctor described him as "masterful in his ways, of persistent combativeness and . . . inclined to be vindictive." Ellen Dent, a wisp of a woman with a twinkle in her gray eyes, countered her husband's surly demeanor with an engaging warmth and southern charm. Together, they raised a family of four sons and three daughters. In 1843, two sons and two daughters still lived at home.

Despite the colonel's gruff attitude, Grant grew to

Head of the Dent family,
Colonel Frederick F. Dent.
(Library of Congress)

enjoy their long talks. One frequent subject of conversation was the issue of slavery. Dent was a confirmed slave owner; Jesse Grant was an outspoken opponent of slavery and Ulysses shared his father's views. He respectfully listened to Dent's opinions, then argued his opposition to slavery calmly and with rare common sense. Ellen Dent admired Grant's firm but quiet ways. Often after Grant had ridden off to return to Jefferson Barracks, her daughters would hear her say: "That young man will be heard from some day. He has a good deal in him. He'll make his mark."

At first, Grant visited the Dents about once a week. In February 1844, however, when the Dents' oldest daughter Julia returned from Miss Mauro's fashionable finishing school in St. Louis, his visits became more frequent. He shyly refused to admit that he was coming by more often. He later remarked: "After that I do not

know that my visits be-
came more frequent; they
certainly did became more
enjoyable."

Julia stood an even five
feet tall with an athletic
figure that some consid-
ered plump. Her long
brown hair framed a
roundish face and expres-
sive brown eyes, one of
which was slightly crossed.
She was not quite a rav-
ishing beauty, but with her
rosy, outdoor complexion

One of the few remaining images of
young Julia Dent.

and keen intellect, she met the world head-on and left
a striking impression on all she met—especially on
young Lieutenant Grant, who courted the energetic
young southern girl for the next several months.

At the end of April, Grant took a short leave to visit
his parents. Four days after he left for Ohio, the 4th
Infantry was ordered to Louisiana, near the Texas bor-
der. Texas had declared its independence from Mexico
and annexation of the Lone Star Republic by the United
States appeared imminent. President John Tyler ordered
the army to the Texas border ostensibly to prevent
American adventurers from fomenting trouble with
Mexico. The president's real reason was to menace the
Mexicans and deter them from intervening in Texas.

Many of Grant's fellow officers were indifferent toward the annexation of Texas, but not him. He was opposed to the move and later recorded his objections this way:

> For myself, I was bitterly opposed to the [annexation] measure, and to this day regard the war [with Mexico], which resulted, as one of the most unjust ever waged by a stronger against a weaker nation. It was an instance of a republic following the bad example of European monarchies, in not considering justice in their desire to acquire additional territory.... Even if the annexation itself could be justified, the manner in which the subsequent war was forced upon Mexico cannot.

Throughout his life, Grant believed that history of the relationship between the United States and Texas—the influx of Americans into a territory belonging to Mexico, its forced separation from Mexico, and its ultimate annexation by the United States—represented part of a conspiracy to acquire additional slave states for the Union. He also believed that the addition of Texas to the Union as a slave state—which happened after the Mexican War—and the potential for acquiring additional slave-holding territory in the West by similar means, encouraged the attempted southern secession of 1861. In Grant's view, the annexation of Texas led to the Mexican War, then to the South's secession, and inevitably to the Civil War. As the good soldier he was, however, he kept his political opinions to himself.

Grant completed his full leave without being recalled to his unit. While away, he could think only of Julia. "I now discovered that I was exceedingly anxious to get back to Jefferson Barracks," he wrote later, "and I understood the reason without explanation from any one." His separation from Julia made him realize that he had fallen in love with her. As for Julia, she later recalled, "I, child that I was, never for a moment thought of him as a lover. But, Oh! How lonely I was without him." When Grant returned, they exchanged tokens of endearment— he gave her his West Point ring in return for a lock of her hair—and they became secretly engaged. Soon afterward, he left for Louisiana.

On June 3, 1844, Grant reported to his regiment near Natchitoches, the oldest town in Louisiana. He found the 4th Infantry quartered in a rough campsite on a high, piney ridge called Camp Salubrity (meaning healthful), about thirty miles from the Texas border. "The great elevation of our situation and the fact that one of the best springs of water in the state puts out here are the only recommendations this place has," Grant noted soon after his arrival. "I have a small tent that the rain runs through as it would through a sieve. The swamps are full of alligators, and the wood full of red bugs and ticks. So much for Camp Salubrity."

Five days after Grant's arrival in Louisiana, the Senate defeated a bill that would have brought Texas into the union. The bill had been pushed by U.S. Secretary of

State John C. Calhoun, a strong proponent of the expansion of slavery who hoped to bring Texas into the Union as a slave state. When Calhoun's resolution was defeated, the tension over possible U.S. intervention in Texas was temporarily relieved. Nevertheless, the 4th Infantry, along with the 3rd Infantry stationed at nearby Fort Jesup, were designated "Corps of Observation," with orders to keep an eye on the border. Brevet Brigadier General Zachary "Old Rough and Ready" Taylor arrived in Louisiana to take charge of the corps, where it—and Grant—remained for the next year.

In November 1844, James K. Polk, of Tennessee, won the presidential election. Polk was an advocate of westward expansion. He had campaigned on the slogan "Fifty-four Forty or Fight," advocating the expansion of America to the latitude 54°54'N, which was then the southern boundary of territory claimed by Russia. The territory below that latitude was also claimed by Great Britain. In an equally zealous move, the lame-duck Tyler administration renewed its effort to annex Texas and succeeded in pushing a joint resolution—which required only a simple majority—through Congress. President John Tyler signed the measure on March 3, 1845, his last day in office, and an offer of statehood was dispatched at once to the Texas capital at Washington-on-the-Brazos. At Camp Salubrity, the Corps of Observation expected action to commence at any moment.

Mexico had refused to recognize Texan independence and still claimed the territory for itself. When news of Tyler's offer arrived, Mexico broke off diplomatic relations with the United States and placed its army on a war footing. Though Mexico would have preferred to have Texas back, it would choose an independent state over one controlled by the U.S. Mexico now offered to recognize the Lone Star Republic if it would remain independent. The Texas Congress took its time mulling both offers.

In April, while Texans considered their destiny, Grant took leave and returned to White Haven to ask Colonel Dent for Julia's hand in marriage. The colonel thought Grant was too poor to consider marriage, but grudgingly left the decision to Julia. Her younger sister, Emma, later pointed out that "it was nonsense for father to be pretending that he had anything to say about it. Julia, having once said Yes, had made his decision for him." The betrothal was no longer secret, but the couple would have a long engagement.

On June 26, 1845, the Texas Congress voted unanimously to join the United States. Three days later, acting Secretary of War George Bancroft directed General Zachary Taylor to occupy a position "on or near the Rio Grande del Norte" that he considered "best adapted to repel invasion." If Texas joined the U.S., it would bring with it a strip of land claimed by both Mexico and Texas. Opinion is still divided over whether Polk sent troops into that area to provoke Mexico to war or, as he claimed, to enforce the Texan claim to that land. In September, the Corps of Observation, renamed the Corps of Occupa-

General Zachary Taylor commanded the American forces as the Mexican War began. *(Library of Congress)*

tion, left New Orleans for Corpus Christi, on the Nueces River in Texas. Shortly thereafter, Grant was promoted to full second lieutenant, with his commission dated back to September 30, the same date his regiment had arrived in Texas.

Reinforcements poured into Corpus Christi over the

winter of 1845–1846. The company officers in Taylor's Corps of Occupation were mostly West Pointers—infantrymen such as Grant, James Longstreet, Winfield Scott Hancock, Simon Bolivar Buckner, and Earl Van Dorn; cavalrymen Albert S. Johnston and Philip Kearny; artillerists Braxton Bragg, George H. Thomas, and Joseph Hooker—all of whom would distinguish themselves in the days ahead. More than half of the enlisted men were foreign-born—forty-two percent Irish or German—but all were regulars: tough, disciplined, and reliable in a fight. "A better army, man for man," Grant wrote later, "probably never faced an enemy than the one commanded by General Taylor in the earliest two engagements of the Mexican war."

As for Taylor himself, he was a gifted commander. Still trim and fit at age sixty-two, he was a proven veteran of the war against Tecumseh (1811), the War of 1812 (1812–1815), the Black Hawk War (1832), and the second Seminole War (1835–1842). Taylor disdained military formality, favoring blue denim pants, a long linen duster, and a large palmetto hat instead of a general's uniform. "He dressed entirely for comfort," Grant noted later, "rarely wearing anything in the field to indicate his rank, or even that he was an officer." A courageous and resourceful leader, Taylor earned the affection of his troops with his modesty and lack of pretension.

On March 11, 1846, General Taylor ordered his army into the arid region between the Nueces River and the Rio Grande—the area claimed by both Texas and Mexico.

Taylor's army of some four thousand regulars reached the Rio Grande on March 28 and established a defensive perimeter across the river from Matamoros. "We were sent to provoke a fight," Grant opined later, "but it was essential that Mexico should commence it." The Americans dug in and built a stronghold that they dubbed Fort Texas, and the military posturing on both sides of the river commenced.

The Mexican War

On April 25, a patrol of General Zachary Taylor's cavalry led by Captain Seth Thornton skirmished with Mexican troops north of the Rio Grande. Sixteen Americans were killed or wounded, and the rest of the patrol were taken prisoner. Taylor notified the government in Washington that "hostilities may now be considered as commenced."

President Polk received Taylor's message on Saturday evening, May 9. On the following Monday, he asked Congress to recognize that "a state of war exists between the Government of the Republic of Mexico and the United States." A half hour later, the House of Representatives voted for war, 173–14; the Senate followed suit the next day, 40–2. The Mexican Congress reciprocated in similar fashion. President Polk formulated a bold offensive strategy: he ordered Taylor's forces on the Rio Grande to invade Mexico. He also directed a contingent of fifteen hundred soldiers under Colonel Stephen W. Kearny and about one thousand Missouri volunteers commanded by Colonel Alexander Doniphan to occupy New Mexico and California. Polk concluded that if U.S. forces occupied the Rio Grande, along with key towns in New Mexico (including present-day Arizona) and California, the Mexicans would be forced to concede defeat and the war would end abruptly. He did not anticipate the tenacious resistance of the Mexicans.

The first major battle was fought on the plain of Palo Alto, near present-day Brownsville, Texas, in the disputed region between the Nueces and the Rio Grande on May 8, 1846—four days before the U.S. Congress officially declared war on Mexico. While protecting his supply line between Fort Texas and Point Isabel, about thirty miles away on the Gulf of Mexico, General Taylor and a contingent of some twenty-three hundred men encountered a Mexican army of about six thousand troops led by General Mariano Arista.

Arista drew his troops, bayonets glistening in the noonday sun, into a line of battle across the road to Matamoros and waited for the advancing Americans. Taylor, calmly and unhurriedly, positioned his regiments in a similar line and signaled them to advance. While moving forward with his regiment, Grant reflected on the loneliness of military command: "I thought what a fearful responsibility General Taylor must feel,

General Taylor leading his troops into battle at Palo Alto. *(Library of Congress)*

commanding such a host and so far from friends."

When the Americans closed to a distance of one thousand yards, Arista's artillery opened fire with mostly four- and eight-pounder cannons firing solid brass shot designed for battering fortifications. Tactically, the solid shot proved ineffective against the Americans, but in human terms it demonstrated its destructive power on an unfortunate few. "A ball struck close by me killing one man instantly," Grant wrote later in a letter to Julia. "It knocked Captain Page's jaw off, and knocked Lt. Wallen and one sergeant down besides, but they were not much hurt. Captain Page is still alive."

Taylor advanced another five hundred yards, then halted his infantry and deployed his artillery— an array of six-pounder cannon and twelve-pounder howitzers— a few paces forward and ordered them to commence firing: "Canister and grape, Major Ringgold. Canister and Grape." (Canister shot was simply lead or iron balls encased in a shell and packed in sawdust; grapeshot was somewhat larger balls fitted into three-layered shells. Both kinds of shot were designed for use against personnel. When the shell exploded, the shot inside flew out, causing even more damage.) The artillery duel raged on until nightfall, when both sides bivouacked and waited for the return of daylight.

At daybreak, Arista withdrew his troops rather than absorb any more punishment. In a battle fought mostly by artillery, the Mexicans suffered losses of over seven hundred killed and wounded, against American losses of fifty-six dead and wounded. The wounded included Major Ringgold, Taylor's brilliant artilleryman, who died a few days later.

This painting depicts the mortal wounding of Major Ringgold at the battle of Palo Alto. *(Library of Congress)*

That afternoon, May 9—the same day that President Polk received news of the initial clash between Thornton's troops and Mexican regulars—General Taylor gave chase to General Arista's fleeing forces. He caught up with them about five miles down the road to Matamoros. Arista had taken advantage of a four-foot-deep dry riverbed to entrench his forces in a natural defensive position. Centuries earlier the Rio Grande had coursed through the ravine, now called Resaca de la Palma. The second battle of the undeclared war commenced there at about 2:00 PM.

Because of the thick chaparral (shrubs) that restricted visibility and therefore the effectiveness of artillery,

After a day of difficult fighting at Palo Alto, Arista withdrew to a more defensible position at Resaca de la Palma, a nearby dry riverbed, to lie in wait for Taylor's troops. The plan to surprise Taylor was thwarted by infighting among the Mexican officers and difficulties in field communication. *(Library of Congress)*

Taylor called on his infantry. What became known as the battle of Resaca de la Palma devolved into a series of savage, hand-to-hand combats involving small parties. At the height of hostilities, Grant led his men through the dense underbrush and captured a wounded Mexican colonel and a few of his men only to discover that they had already been captured. "This left no doubt in my mind but that the battle of Resaca de la Palma would have been won, just as it was," he recalled later, "if I had not been there."

Notwithstanding Grant's wry recollection, the battle of Resaca de la Palma was fought with murderous intensity for several hours until Arista's troops, already demoralized by their defeat at Palo Alto, broke and ran. Many Mexicans drowned attempting to cross the Rio Grande, in addition to the more than seven hundred killed, wounded, captured, or missing. The Americans suffered losses of just over one hundred killed and wounded. In a letter to a family friend in Ohio, Grant—now a blooded veteran—described his feelings on the battlefield: "I do not know that I felt any peculiar sensation. War seems much less horrible to persons engaged in it than to those who read of the battles."

In the meantime, while Taylor's forces had been battling to protect their supply line, the Mexicans had attacked Fort Texas. Under its commander Major Jacob Brown, the fort had beat back its attackers—at the cost of Brown's life and that of one other soldier. The Americans renamed the post Fort Brown. Across the river, the remnants of Arista's army evacuated Matamoros a week later and faded into the hills. Taylor crossed the Rio Grande on May 18 and set up his headquarters outside the town. He paused there and later at his advanced base at Camargo, some seventy miles farther west, to reinforce his ranks and to replenish his equipment and supplies. Camargo was an unhealthy town sunk in mud from a recent flooding and beset with 112-degree heat and disease. By August, Taylor had assembled a force of fifteen thousand troops, but many of the new arrivals fell sick, and he had to leave them behind when he resumed his campaign.

On August 18, 1846, Taylor, with a force of some six thousand men—about half regulars and half short-term volunteers—began a southward drive aimed at capturing the Mexican fortress city of Monterrey. Taylor calculated that whichever army owned Monterrey owned northern Mexico. At about the same time, Grant was appointed, much to his dismay, quartermaster and commissary officer of the 4th Infantry. He considered the assignment an attempt to deprive him of his fair share of the action because his position was largely administrative. In reality, he was the right man for the job. Keeping the troops supplied and fed was perhaps the most important job in the army. Moreover, in the execution of his new duties, Grant would gain invaluable experience that would serve him well in the troubled years to come.

Taylor's forces reached Monterrey on September 19.

The battle of Monterrey was characterized by three days of vicious street fighting.
(Library of Congress)

They found a city of stone built in a pass of the Sierra Madre. The Santa Catarina River effectively shielded its southern exposure. Forts and other fortifications protected the northern and eastern approaches to the city, while two fortified heights straddled the road to Saltillo in the west. Within the citadel-like city of stone houses and barricaded streets, General Pedro de Ampudia, who had replaced the humiliated Arista, commanded a force of seven thousand men and forty guns against Taylor's six thousand attackers. The battle of Monterrey (September 20–25, 1846) would be particularly bloody.

On September 20, Taylor split his forces, sending a two thousand-man detachment of regulars and Texas cavalry under General William J. Worth to attack the city from the west, while he himself led an assault from the east. Worth succeeded in capturing the key defensive position on Federation Hill on September 21, and secured Independence Hill the next day. Meanwhile, in the east, Taylor's contingent—including the 4th Infantry led by Grant's commander Lieutenant Colonel John Garland—drove the Mexican garrison into a stronghold in the center of the city called the Citadel and laid siege to it.

Grant, who as quartermaster had been left behind to guard the regiment's camp and supplies when his unit advanced, could not contain his curiosity and rode to the sound of the guns to see what was happening. Just as he arrived at the scene of the action, his unit launched its attack. Grant later explained that, "lacking the moral courage to return to camp—where I had been ordered to stay—I charged with the regiment."

The next day found him again with his regiment in the thick of the action pinned down by Mexican sharpshooters in the town plaza. When ammunition ran low in the 3rd and 4th Infantry regiments, Grant—one of the few soldiers with a horse—volunteered to ride back to their supply point to call for more munitions. Hooking one leg over the cantle (rear projection) of his saddle and one arm around his horse's neck, and draping his body down the sheltered side of the animal, Grant galloped "Indian fashion" through the streets of the besieged city under a torrent of Mexican fire. Grant delivered his commander's message with neither horse nor rider receiving a scratch. Typically subdued, he later shrugged off his perilous ride as nothing extraordinary. After all, he pointed out, only the far side of his horse had been exposed to danger.

After three days of house-to-house street fighting, General Ampudia, recognizing that his forces were effectively surrounded, offered to quit fighting on condition that his troops be allowed to pull out of town with all their arms and equipment. Ampudia also proposed a temporary truce to take immediate effect. Taylor agreed to Ampudia's conditions, believing that a gracious acceptance of his terms would advance peace negotiations already begun between President Polk and Mexican President General Antonio López de Santa Anna. Hostilities ceased momentarily.

The American dead included Lieutenant Charles Hoskins, the regimental adjutant and a friend of Grant's. In addition to his quartermaster duties, Grant now took

After the costly battle at Monterrey, General Ampudia tendered his surrender to General Scott on September 24, 1846. *(Library of Congress)*

over as adjutant of the 4th Infantry. After nightfall on the day of Hoskins's death, Grant returned to the battlefield in the pouring rain to identify the body. Lieutenant Calvin Benjamin, of the 4th Artillery, found Grant beside the body of his dead friend, lifting the head of a wounded man and "giving him water from a canteen and wiping his face with a moistened handkerchief."

At battle's end, Grant weighed the implications of General Taylor's acceptance of General Ampudia's ceasefire conditions and filed away his conclusions in the repository of his mind. Taylor's magnanimity toward his opponent might have influenced Grant's own generosity in accepting another foe's surrender years later at Appomattox. At the time, however, in a letter to Julia, Grant confided that he wished the recent battle would be his last: "I hope it may be so for fighting is no longer a pleasure." He had lost many friends at Monterrey, including a half dozen from Jefferson Barracks.

As a wartime quartermaster, Grant participated in a wide range of duties. One of his most important—and dangerous—jobs was supervising ambulance operations and evacuating the wounded under fire. Most of the wounded could be found where the action was heaviest, which was also where Grant could be found— tending to the wounded and gaining a broad perspective of the entire battlefront. "He could see the whole line," his friend James Longstreet commented later, "and knew all that was going on by personal inspection."

With three battles behind him, Grant no doubt expected to continue serving under General Taylor as "Old Zack" pressed deeper into Mexico, but politics intervened. Although Grant and many of his fellow officers supported Taylor's acceptance of Ampudia's surrender at Monterrey, President Polk did not. He was incensed that Taylor had allowed Ampudia's army to escape and ordered the armistice terminated. The president also suspected that Taylor held presidential ambitions of his own, which would be enhanced by Taylor's recent victories in Mexico. Without informing Taylor—either by oversight or design—Polk entrusted the final victory in Mexico to General Winfield Scott, the army's commanding general. Both Scott and Taylor were members of the Whig party, and both men entertained presidential aspirations, but Polk, a Democrat, decided that Scott posed a lesser political threat. As a result of Polk's political machinations, most of Taylor's troops, including Grant's regiment, were reassigned to General Scott's command.

When it came to leadership style, the flamboyant Scott—Old Fuss and Feathers—was the exact opposite of the low-key Taylor, but both generals were gifted commanders. Scott had opposed the U.S. strategy of invading northern Mexico from the start. He felt that victory lay in a seaborne operation aimed at capturing Mexico City. The fall of the Mexican capital, he thought, would bring a quick end to the war. He worked out a strategy to accomplish his aim.

While Scott prepared to invade Mexico near Veracruz, Mexican President Santa Anna got wind of Scott's plan and devised a bold plan of his own: with a reassembled army of some twenty thousand troops, he would first defeat Taylor's remaining forces in the north, then turn southward to repel Scott's invaders. After a long forced march, Santa Anna's army engaged what remained of Taylor's forces—about six thousand troops—at Buena Vista. After a two-day battle (February 22–23, 1847), in which West Point graduate Colonel Jefferson Davis led his Mississippi Volunteers in a pivotal counterattack, Santa Anna called off his attack and returned to Mexico City to prepare for Scott's impending invasion. The battle, which effectively ended the fighting in northern Mexico, cost Santa Anna fifteen hundred casualties; U.S. losses numbered nearly eight hundred. Unfortunately for President Polk, Taylor's victory at Buena Vista would virtually assure his successful bid for the presidency in 1848.

On March 5, 1847, General Scott's fleet carrying some twelve thousand American troops—now renamed the "Army of Invasion"—appeared off Veracruz. Four days later, Scott conducted the first large-scale amphibious landing in the history of the U.S. Army, on a long white beach about four miles south of the key Mexican seaport. For whatever reason, the Mexicans did not offer resistance, and the Americans completed an encirclement of the city on March 14. Instead of mounting a direct assault on the walled city, as Taylor had done at Monterrey, Scott laid siege to the city, vowing not to lose more than one hundred men in capturing it. "For every

General Scott and his troops landed on the beaches near Veracruz after making their way down Mexico's gulf coast.

one over that number I shall regard myself as his murderer," he declared. Grant noted the contrast in strategy and learned another valuable lesson that would bear future rewards.

After a six-day bombardment by naval guns and mortars, Veracruz and its fortress across the bay at San Juan de Ulúa capitulated on March 27. General Scott entered the city two days later and began preparing for a march on Mexico City, almost three hundred miles to the west. Scott's first triumph of the war cost him nineteen dead and sixty-three wounded; the defenders suffered eighty military and one hundred civilian casualties.

On April 8, eager to leave Veracruz before the yellow fever, or *vómito*, season arrived, Scott designated Jalapa—a city in the highlands on the old National Road about seventy-four miles inland—as his next objective. The lead elements of Scott's corps encountered the enemy at Cerro Gordo, a fortified mountain pass about fifty miles along the road to Jalapa. Grant later offered this description of the defile: "Cerro Gordo is one of the higher spurs of the mountains some twelve to fifteen miles east of Jalapa, and Santa Anna had selected this point as the easiest to defend against an invading army. The road, said to have been built by Cortez, zigzags around the mountain-side and was defended at every turn by artillery. On either side were deep chasms or mountain walls. A direct attack along the road was an impossibility. A flank movement seemed equally impossible."

The Americans bivouacked on the Plan del Rio, about three miles short of the pass. Scott ordered his engineers, under the direction of Captain Robert E. Lee, to conduct reconnaissance of the area and to find a way around. Lee's subordinate engineers included a number of officers who would gain high rank and renown in the great civil conflict to come, such as Lieutenants Pierre G. T. Beauregard and George B. McClellan. On April 16, Lee himself found a little-used mountain trail and set his engineers to work making it passable for the rest of the corps. Over the next two days, Scott deployed his artillery to the rear of Santa Anna's fortifications and launched his attack on April 18.

"The surprise of the enemy was complete, the victory overwhelming," Grant penned later. "Some three thousand prisoners fell into Scott's hands, also a large amount of ordnance and ordnance stores. The prisoners were paroled, the artillery parked and ammunition destroyed." In fierce fighting, much of it hand-to-hand, the Americans swept through the pass and forced Santa Anna to flee back to Mexico City. Scott's crushing victory at Cerro Gordo came at cost of almost four hundred Americans killed and wounded. Santa Anna lost 204 officers

American troops raise their hats to General Scott after his stunning victory at the battle of Cerro Gordo.

and 2,837 men by capture alone, along with forty-three guns and four thousand small arms.

The battle of Cerro Gordo (April 18, 1847) was a textbook triumph that induced Grant to see Scott in a new light. In the flamboyant general, he now saw a commander of extraordinary brilliance. He marveled that, "The attack was made as ordered, and perhaps there was not a battle of the Mexican War, or of any other, where orders issued before an engagement were nearer being a correct report of what afterwards took place." Grant's apprenticeship in learning the art of war continued under a master of the game, whom he respected but did not particularly like.

After Scott's victory at Cerro Gordo, he pressed on to Jalapa and paused there for a month to recover and resupply. Continuing his offensive, Scott reached Puebla on May 29, at which point he recognized that the enlistments of thousands of his short-term volunteers were about to expire. He paused again, living off the land while awaiting reinforcements and more supplies to pour in. Two months later, Scott's army had regained a strength of some ten thousand men, and Scott resumed his march toward the Mexican capital. The fight for Mexico City began in mid-August with a series of battles at Contreras, Churubusco, and Chapultepec.

On August 10, Scott and his forces arrived at Ayolta, a town located on a high plateau about fourteen miles from Mexico City. By then, Santa Anna had concentrated twenty thousand troops, chiefly at Contreras and

Churubusco, to guard the southern approaches to the capital. The direct road ahead entered the city from the east and was barred by heavily fortified positions. Captain Robert E. Lee worked another miracle and found a mule path that outflanked the Mexican positions in the southern lake district and came out at Contreras. On August 19, Scott sent an American detachment of thirty-three hundred men under Brevet Major General Gideon J. Pillow to attack the village held by General Gabriel Valencia, but the Mexicans repulsed Pillow's initial assault. The following day, however, Pillow's forces routed the five thousand Mexican defenders, killing seven hundred and capturing eight hundred, while taking only sixty casualties of their own.

Heartened by his success at Contreras, Scott pursued Valencia's fleeing forces that same day to Churubusco, where Santa Anna had shifted a large segment of his defenders. The Mexicans set up a strong fortification at a bridge before the town, and converted a thick-walled church and a massive stone convent into fortresses. When the Americans arrived on August 20, the Mexicans greeted them with heavy musket and cannon fire and fought as never before. Scott's men regained the initiative in midafternoon, partly because the Mexicans were running low on ammunition, and the Americans ultimately carried the day. Santa Anna later admitted that the battle for Churubusco had cost him about a third of his army. Scott's losses totaled more than a thousand killed and wounded.

Scott, with his army undefeated in several battles and now positioned five miles from Mexico City, proposed an armistice to consider peace terms. Santa Anna accepted and fighting was suspended on August 24. But the peace talks collapsed two weeks later, and Scott resumed his offensive on September 8.

Scott's principal objective now was the Castle of Chapultepec, home of Mexico's National Military Academy, which stood on a rocky, walled hill of the same name, high above the plain about three miles southwest of the city. First, however, Scott sent General Worth and his troops to create a diversion at an array of low stone buildings, a half mile west of Chapultepec. The buildings known as El Molino del Rey (or the King's Mill) allegedly housed a cannon foundry. After an all-day battle, Worth's contingent overran the heavily defended mill and inflicted heavy casualties on the defenders—but at a high cost in American lives. Grant distinguished himself in the battle, helping to position American light-artillery effectively, and later storming the mill, which turned out to be only a grain storehouse.

At 8:00 AM on September 13, following an artillery barrage from his twenty-four-pounder guns, Scott launched a three-pronged attack over the causeways leading to Chapultepec Hill. Braving a blizzard of fire from above, the U.S. 3rd and 4th Divisions, led by Generals Gideon Pillow and John Quitman, respectively, scaled the heights and overran the castle by 9:30 AM. With hardly a pause, Scott pressed his attack across the

From a church belfry, Grant's men were able to fire on the police station below during the taking of Mexico City. This painting shows Grant directing their fire. *(Library of Congress)*

causeways leading to the Belén and San Cosmé *garitas* (stone police/customs stations) on the city's west side.

During the assault on the San Cosmé *garita*, Grant again did himself proud. He hauled a small howitzer to the flat roof of a church belfry and directed punishing fire on the *garita*, then returned to ground level to engage in the savage street fighting. By evening, General Worth's 1st Division and Quitman's 4th Division had stormed and taken the two western *garitas*. Working through the night with picks and crowbars, the Americans hacked their way through the walls and entered the capital on September 14.

Scott's troops, exhausted and depleted by some eight hundred casualties from the previous day's fighting, now faced the unenviable task of having to clear the city in house-to-house fighting. This was averted when the Mexicans surrendered their capital at first light. On September 15, General Winfield Scott, after having waged a near-perfect campaign, joined his troops in the city and slept that night in the National Palace, where a contingent of United States Marines stood guard.

Over the course of his campaign from Veracruz to Mexico City, General Scott demonstrated his brilliance on the field of combat. He displayed personal courage, near-flawless leadership, and professionalism. Captain Robert E. Lee said, "He sees everything and counts the cost of every measure." Scott himself ascribed his success to the West Pointers in his army, but Grant accorded Scott his well-deserved due: "Credit is due to the troops engaged, it is true, but the plans and strategy were the general's."

On September 16, two days after the fighting ceased, Grant was promoted to the permanent rank of first lieutenant. He also received two retroactive temporary

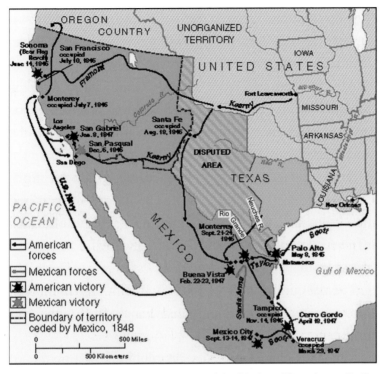

This map shows the contested territories of the Mexican War, along with the critical moves and battles of the opposing armies.

promotions for bravery under fire: to brevet first lieutenant (September 8, 1847) "for gallant and meritorious conduct in the Battle of Molino del Rey"; and to brevet captain (September 13, 1847) for similar conduct during the assault on the San Cosmé *garita*. (In those days, the army awarded temporary promotions in lieu of medals for bravery in combat actions.)

The Treaty of Guadalupe Hidalgo, signed by both nations on February 2, 1848, essentially ended the Mexican War, but the two nations did not ratify the treaty until May 30. And the last American soldier did not quit

Mexican soil and embark for home until August 1, 1848. Brevet Captain U. S. Grant was among the last to leave, departing with the 4th Infantry on July 16.

At war's end, in a letter to Julia, Grant summed up his thoughts on the American march to Mexico City: "Since my last letter four of the hardest fought battles that the world has ever witnessed have taken place, and the most astonishing victories have crowned the American arms. But dearly have they paid for it. The loss of officers and men killed and wounded is frightful. . . . [O]ut of all the officers that left Jefferson Barracks with the 4th Infantry, only three besides myself now remain with us."

Twenty-one officers of the 4th Infantry had left with the regiment in 1844; only four, including Grant, returned in 1848.

The Mexican War holds the dubious distinction of having established the highest percentage of soldiers killed of any American war. It was in this bloody laboratory that Ulysses S. Grant and his contemporaries learned the science of modern warfare. Less than thirteen years after the end of the Mexican War, they would be called upon again to practice their bitterly acquired skills.

Depression to Secession

On July 23, 1848, the 4th Infantry arrived in Pascagoula, Mississippi, where it was to spend the rest of the summer, and Grant applied for and received a two-month leave of absence. Booking passage on the first available riverboat heading north, he arrived in St. Louis five days later. He had waited four and a half years to make Julia Dent his bride and was determined to wait no longer. The seasoned captain of infantry and his fiancée at last exchanged wedding vows in the Dent family's townhouse in St. Louis on August 22. Julia's cousin, James Longstreet, served as Grant's best man; his messmate, Cadmus Wilcox, and Bernard Pratte III of St. Louis assisted as ushers. All three fellow officers would keep a future date with Grant at Appomattox Court House in April 1865. In his *Memoirs*, written years

Ulysses and Julia in 1848, the year they were wed.

later, Grant commented only briefly on the wedding: "I was married to Miss Julia Dent, the lady of whom I have before spoken."

The captain and his bride left right after the nuptials to visit Grant's parents in Ohio. The Grants welcomed Julia in their plain, low-key style, but inherent differences in their lifestyles would eventually cast a shadow over their relationship. "They considered me ' unpardonably extravagant," Julia said, "and I considered them inexcuseably the other way."

On November 17, the newlyweds journeyed to Detroit, Michigan, where Grant reported to the new headquarters of the 4th Infantry. To his surprise, he learned he had been assigned to duty at the bleak army outpost at Madison Barracks in Sackets Harbor, New York, on the eastern shores of Lake Ontario. They spent the winter in one of the coldest places in the eastern United States. Grant applied for and received a transfer back to Detroit, but his reassignment had to wait until April of 1849 when the spring thaw melted the snows and ice enough to allow travel.

In April 1849, they rented a comfortable five-room frame house in Detroit. Julia took advantage of Grant's transfer to visit her parents at White Haven. By the time she joined her husband in July, he had settled in to his new duties, "where," he recalled later, "two years were spent with but few important incidents." One of the most important of those incidents occurred the following spring when Julia gave birth to a son named Frederick Dent Grant in honor of Julia's father.

The Grants enjoyed their stay in Detroit and the mostly uneventful two years passed quickly. In the spring of 1851, the Detroit garrison was reassigned to

The Grants' house at 253 Ford Street in Detroit. *(Library of Congress)*

Madison Barracks in Sackets Harbor, and a year after that, Grant's entire regiment was ordered to the Pacific Coast. The move would entail a passage by ship from New York to Panama, an overland trek across the dangerous, disease-ridden jungles of the Panamanian isthmus, and a second shipboard transit from Panama to San Francisco (the Panama Canal would not officially open until 1914). Julia, now eight months pregnant with their second child, wanted to accompany her husband, but Grant would not hear of it. "You know how loath I am to leave you," he said, "but crossing Panama is an undertaking for one in robust health." Julia finally agreed to go to White Haven to have her baby, and Grant set out alone, promising to send for her and the children as soon as possible.

On July 5, 1852, Grant boarded the steamer *Ohio* at Governor's Island, New York. The *Ohio* anchored off Aspinwall (now Colón) on July 16 and the 4th Infantry, and some family members, disembarked and began its westward trek across the steamy Isthmus of Panama at the height of the wet season. The regiment soon found itself wallowing along slick and muddy trails, assailed by tropical downpours and the searing summer sun; soon they were dealing with a cholera epidemic. Grant's duties as regimental quartermaster required him to bring up the rear of the column and supervise government and public properties of the seven hundred men, women, and children.

Driving cantankerous mules through the jungle in a

race against disease—cholera claimed another victim every hour—Grant survived the ordeal that he later described as having cost the lives of about "one-seventh of those who left New York harbor with the 4th Infantry on July 5." He likely owed his life to a self-imposed regimen of avoiding all water—even to bathe in—and drinking only wine, a discipline that he recommended to soldiers and civilians alike. Most soldiers heeded his advice; many civilians did not. Meanwhile, at White Haven, Julia gave birth to their second son, Ulysses Jr.— whom they would call Buck—on July 22, 1852.

In early August, the regiment reached Panama City on the Pacific Coast and set sail for San Francisco aboard a steamship appropriately named *Golden Gate*. While steaming past Acapulco, Grant wrote to Julia about his regiment's travail in Panama. "My dearest," he wrote, "you could never have crossed the Isthmus at this season. . . . The horrors . . . are beyond description. . . . I will say however that there is a great accountability some where for the loss which we have sustained." Grant clearly felt distressed over his inability to keep all of his stricken party alive.

On the evening of August 17, the *Golden Gate* tied up at San Francisco's long wharf and Grant stepped into a city bustling with gold seekers and the legion of entrepreneurs, merchants, hustlers, gamblers, and swindlers dedicated to separating the gold from its finders. Caught up in the excitement, he fell in love with the state. He was not alone: California's population had grown

This engraving of the bustling port of San Francisco was made not long after Grant's arrival. *(Library of Congress)*

from twenty thousand in 1848 to 225,000 in 1852, with another fifty thousand arriving annually. He wrote Julia that California was beyond the wildest dreams of people "in the states," adding, "There is no reason why an active, energetic person should not make a fortune a year." But fortunes somehow managed to always elude him.

The army sent the 4th Infantry to Benicia Barracks near San Francisco for a few weeks of rest before assigning its members to various garrison posts. Grant himself was posted to Fort Vancouver, Oregon (later Washington) Territory. He reported there on September 20, and with vast energies and an ill-fated entrepreneurial spirit, he set about trying to make his fortune in off-duty hours. Grant hoped to bring his family west but could not afford to do so on his salary. Consequently, he developed a

Located on the beautiful banks of the Columbia River, Fort Vancouver was home to a flourishing fur trade, among other blossoming industries, during the nineteenth century. The distant peak in this picture's background is Mount Hood. *(University of Washington Library Archives)*

passion for making money and attempted a series of unsuccessful ventures, such as shipping cattle and pigs to San Francisco in partnership with his friend, Lieutenant Henry Wallen. The result of their enterprise was typical of Grant's moneymaking schemes. "We continued that business," Wallen said later, "until both of us lost all the money we had."

On September 30, 1853, Grant received word that he had been promoted to the permanent rank of captain on the previous August 5, as a replacement for an officer who had died. (Promotions were slow to come in the peacetime army, which had been severely reduced in size after the Mexican War.) Along with the promotion came a transfer to Fort Humboldt, California, to assume command of the 4th Infantry's F Company. Even with

Grant's small pay increase, he still could not send for his family. "A cook could not be hired for the pay of a captain," Grant often said. "The cook could do better."

Grant's duties as an infantry company commander at Fort Humboldt were fewer and less time-consuming than his previous responsibilities as a regimental quartermaster. With more time on his hands, his continued isolation and separation from his family began to weigh heavily on him. Adding to his mounting woes, his commanding officer, Brevet Lieutenant Colonel Robert C. Buchanan, was a competent officer but a strict disciplinarian who made life difficult for his subordinates. Grant sank into a sea of despondency and sought refuge—as did many regular army officers of the day—in alcohol. He wrote Julia, "How forsaken I feel here."

In the nineteenth century, alcohol, and alcoholism, was a huge presence in the United States—especially in the military. Grant began to drink because of his loneliness and his boredom with military life. But drinking only further depressed him and soon began to affect his performance. Grant, it appears, had a very low tolerance for alcohol—likely because of his small size. Only two or three drinks might make him appear very intoxicated. The problem came, however, when his drinking interfered with his work. He soon realized this and even attempted to join the Sons of Temperance while in Sackets Harbor. That attempt to stop drinking failed.

What was perhaps Grant's low point came during his time at Fort Humboldt. Buchanan, Grant's commander, had seen Grant under the influence of alcohol and began to suspect his judgment. Matters came to a head one day in the spring of 1854 when Grant, drunk, was unable to competently handle his payroll duties. Colonel Buchanan gave him the option of standing trial by court-martial or resigning his commission. Grant chose to resign rather than let Julia share in his humiliation—and he kept the truth of the matter to himself. "I saw no chance of supporting them [his family] on the Pacific coast out of my pay as an army officer," he wrote later. "I concluded, therefore, to resign." Though Grant would never again be dominated by alcohol the way he was in California, he had gained a reputation that he would not easily shake. Rumors about his drinking would follow him for the rest of his life.

Grant arrived back in New York—again via the Isthmus of Panama—on June 25, 1854, virtually penniless. With financial aid from Simon Bolivar Buckner, his fellow officer and friend since West Point, he stayed in New York briefly before heading home on money borrowed from his father. His resignation became effective of July 31, 1854. At age thirty-two, he was no longer Captain Grant. Now he had to face, in his words, "a new struggle for our support." As the next seven years would show, "struggle" was an understatement.

Grant first turned to farming to make a living. Julia owned sixty acres on the Dent estate, a wedding gift from her father, but the land had no house and it needed to be cleared. Moreover, Grant had no money for seed and farm implements, and Julia was pregnant with their third child Ellen—whom they called "Nellie"—was born on July 4, 1855. The family initially stayed with the Dents at White Haven, and then they moved into a house that Julia's brother Louis had built nearby called Wish-ton-wish, a word borrowed from Native Americans, which the family believed meant "whippoorwill." Grant worked long and hard to build a house and clear their land, gradually inching toward his goal of becoming a prosperous farmer.

Julia owned three slaves, which never sat well with Grant. To help him in the fields, he hired free blacks and paid them more than the prevailing wage. One of Grant's workers, a freedmen called Uncle Jason, later explained, "Some of the white men cussed about it," but Grant stuck to his course.

Mary Jackson, one of Colonel Dent's house servants at White Haven, remembered Grant as being not only "the kindest husband and the most indulgent father I ever saw," but also as "a very kind man to those who worked for him and he always said he wanted to give his wife's slaves their freedom as soon as he was able." Grant knew this would not sit well with Colonel Dent, which made him all the more determined to finish building his house and achieve a semblance of independence from his blustery father-in-law.

The Grants moved into their new home in the summer of 1856. In a rural setting where almost all the farms had names, most of them grandiloquent, Grant named his

Hardscrabble, the house that Grant built with his own hands.

small place Hardscrabble. In the fall, the squire of
Hardscrabble cast his first vote in a presidential election. Because he was convinced that the election of a
Republican president would provoke the Southern slave
states into seceding from the Union, Grant voted for
Democrat James Buchanan. "With a Democrat elected
by a unanimous vote of the Slave States, there could be
no pretext for secession for four years," he wrote in his
Memoirs. "I very much hoped that the passions of the
people would subside in that time, and the catastrophe
be averted altogether." During the ensuing four years,
Grant's hope for himself was to escape from poverty, but
fortune continued to work against him.

The Panic of 1857, which was initiated by the rail-

roads defaulting on their bonds and the resultant de-
valuation of railroad stocks, forced banks to close and
crop prices to wither. Grant's finances withered with
them. Just before Christmas that year, he pawned his
watch for twenty-two dollars so that his family would
have presents on Christmas morning.

In the spring of 1858, Julia gave birth to their third
son and last child, Jesse Root Grant Jr. At about the same
time, Grant fell ill with ague (a fever, such as malaria,
that is accompanied by sudden fits of chills and sweat-
ing), which rendered him unfit to continue farming. That
fall, he sold out his stock, crops, and farming utensils—
and later his farm. With the help of the Dents, Grant next
established a real-estate partnership with Julia's cousin
Harry Boggs. But the business did not bring in enough

The Grant family *(left to right)*: Fred, Jesse, Julia, Ulysses Jr. (Buck), Ulysses, and
Nellie. *(National Portrait Gallery, Washington, D.C.)*

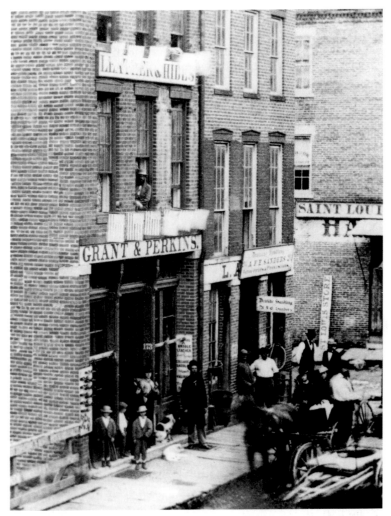

The Grant & Perkins leather shop in Galena, where Grant was able to work for his father during tough financial times.

earnings to support two families, so Grant applied for a position as county engineer. When the position went to a rival candidate, primarily because the appointing politicians preferred a Republican, Grant decided to withdraw from his real-estate partnership and to accept

73

a clerkship in his father's leather-goods store in Galena, Illinois.

Grant moved his family to Galena in May 1860. The curious career of Sam Grant had come full circle—from obscurity on the Ohio River to a warrior's apprenticeship at West Point on the Hudson; to fields of battle where he had distinguished himself from the Rio Grande to Mexico City; to the shores of the far Pacific where he had fought depression and intemperance; and finally to a tiny town on the upper Mississippi where, as a lowly clerk, he appeared to be slipping back into obscurity. Had he died in 1860, his life's passage would be forgotten in time.

In the autumn of the fateful year of 1860, American voters elected antislavery Republican candidate Abraham Lincoln to the presidency of the United States. Contrary to Grant's hope that "the passions of the people would subside" during four years of a Buchanan administration, they had not. Lincoln had repeatedly promised to not interfere where slavery currently existed, but to stop it from expanding into the west, while Southern leaders were convinced that if slavery could not expand it would die. Shortly after Lincoln's election, eleven Southern states seceded from the Union and organized the Confederate States of America (CSA) and elected former West Pointer and Mexican War hero Jefferson Davis as the first president.

Lincoln was determined to preserve the Union; war seemed inevitable. On April 12, 1861, barely a month

after the new president's inaugural, Confederate artillery fired on U.S. soldiers stationed at Fort Sumter, in
the harbor of Charleston, South Carolina. The catastrophe that Grant had so long feared had begun.

THE NORTH AND THE SOUTH

While there were many social and cultural differences between
the Northern and Southern states previous to the American Civil War
(1861–1865), the issue that brought the young nation to war was the
conflict over the expansion of slavery. Slave-holding Southerners, a
minority of the population, wanted to extend slavery to Kansas and
other western territories; most Northerners believed the new territories and states should be reserved for independent farmers and
free laborers. Proslavery advocates realized that if slavery did not
expand, the slave states would eventually be outnumbered in Congress and slavery would be eradicated by law. As Abraham Lincoln
said frequently in his speeches, slavery in the original Southern states
was, regrettably, protected in the Constitution, but at some future
date, if no more slave states were allowed to enter the union, it would
be possible to legally end it through an act of Congress or the passage
of a Constitutional amendment.

Lincoln was elected president on November 6, 1860. On the
following December 6, South Carolina seceded from the Union. Six
more states in the deep South followed South Carolina's lead in quick
succession—Mississippi, Florida, Alabama, Georgia, Louisiana, and
Texas. Representatives of these seven states met in Montgomery,
Alabama, on February 8, 1861, and formed a new federation called
the Confederate States of America. The Confederacy elected Jefferson
Davis—a former secretary of war and member of both houses of
Congress—as its president on February 9, 1861.

On March 4, 1861, Abraham Lincoln took the oath of office
as the sixteenth president of the United States and declared secession

illegal. Following the Confederate firing on Fort Sumter, South Carolina, on April 12, he called three days later for a volunteer army to put down what he referred to as the rebellion. After this call for troops four more Southern states joined the Confederacy—Virginia, Arkansas, North Carolina, and Tennessee—to up the total of secessionist states to eleven.

Twenty-five states stayed with or joined the Union during hostilities—California, Connecticut, Delaware, Illinois, Indiana, Iowa, Kansas, Kentucky, Maine, Maryland, Massachusetts, Michigan, Minnesota, Missouri, Nevada (1864 statehood), New Hampshire, New Jersey, New York, Ohio, Oregon, Pennsylvania, Rhode Island, Vermont, West Virginia (1863 statehood), and Wisconsin. Of the twenty-five, Delaware, Maryland, Kentucky, and Missouri were slave-holding border states; the latter three held divided loyalties.

5

Grant Takes Command

On April 15, 1861, the day after the surrender of Fort Sumter, President Abraham Lincoln called for seventy-five thousand volunteers to serve for ninety days, which he felt would be long enough to stifle "combinations too powerful to be suppressed by the ordinary course of judicial proceedings." (Lincoln consistently refused to recognize the Confederacy as a legitimate government and always referred to the conflict as an illegal revolt.) Shortly afterward, the president issued a proclamation convening a special session of Congress to put the nation on a war footing. When news of Lincoln's first call for volunteers reached Galena, the townspeople offered Grant command of the rapidly formed Galena company. Grant declined their offer, candidly explaining, "I think I can serve the State better at Springfield [the state capital]." He thought that if he entered the conflict, it should not be at the head of a local group of volunteers. Considering his West Point training and eleven years of service in the army, he believed that he was qualified to command a regiment.

He did, however, agree to train the company, which later became Company F of the 12th Illinois Infantry. With the leadership skills of a former infantry commander and the organizational talents of a past regimental quartermaster, Grant readied the town's rifle company for service in a week. When Galena's volunteers marched off to the train depot to leave for Springfield, Grant, shabbily dressed in civilian clothes and carrying a battered carpetbag, fell in behind the last rank and marched with it to the station and began his journey to immortality.

After the Galena company was mustered into state service in late April, Grant was preparing to return home when Illinois governor Richard Yates, who was acting on a recommendation from Galena Congressman Elihu Washburne, asked him to help the state's adjutant general raise and organize sixteen regiments. Grant spent the next month as mustering officer, working out of an unused anteroom in the adjutant's office with a generous supply of cigars.

While in Springfield, Grant met Captain John Pope, an old friend from West Point who had served on General Taylor's staff in Mexico. Pope, who was from a wealthy family, was awaiting a political appointment to brigadier general. He urged Grant to return to the army right away and offered to use his influence among Illinois politicians to help Grant get a commission. Grant turned down his friend's offer, later explaining, "I declined to receive endorsement for permission to fight for my country." Acting on his own, Grant offered his

John Pope. *(Library of Congress)*

services to Brevet Brigadier Lorenzo Thomas, the army's adjutant general, and also to Major General George B. McClellan, commander of the Department of Ohio. In the confused run-up to war, neither general responded to Grant's offer.

As part of his duties, Grant mustered in the 21st Illinois Infantry at Mattoon, eighty miles east of Springfield, in early May. Despite his stooped posture, cheap suit of clothes, and soft black hat, he impressed the officers of the regiment. "Anyone who looked beyond that [his appearance] recognized that he was a professional soldier," said Lieutenant Joseph Vance. A month later, just as Grant began to resign himself to sitting out the war, Governor Yates appointed him colonel in command of the 21st Illinois, to replace the regiment's original commander, who had been unable to maintain discipline.

Grant took command of the regiment on June 15, 1861, and issued his first order three days later: "In accepting this command, your Commander will require the cooperation of all the commissioned and noncommissioned officers . . . and hopes to receive also the hearty support of every enlisted man." He recognized the importance of insisting on cooperation from his unit leaders and in earning the respect of his rank-and-file soldiers. On June 28, Grant and his regiment—thirty-six officers and slightly more than nine hundred enlisted men—were mustered into Federal service.

In the first weeks of the war, most of the concern was in keeping the so-called border states from seceding. Kentucky was one of the most important. Initially, state leaders attempted, unrealistically, to remain neutral. Lincoln was determined to keep his birth state solidly in the Union.

Kentucky, a mountainous state, served as a barrier between what came to be the eastern and a western theaters of the war. Troops from Ohio and Indiana covered most of the Appalachian sector, including Kentucky. Troops from Illinois and Iowa took responsibility for securing Missouri, another border state with deeply divided sympathies. On July 3, 1861, Grant's regiment was ordered to Quincy, Illinois, 116 miles west of Springfield, across the Mississippi River from Missouri. That same day, the state of Illinois was transferred to the War Department's newly established Western Department and placed under the command of renowned western explorer and former presidential candidate Major General John C. Fremont. Nine days later, Grant crossed into Missouri with orders to guard the Hannibal and St. Joseph railroad, which was being menaced by a pro-Secessionist Missouri State Guard division commanded by Confederate General Thomas A. Harris.

On July 17, Grant advanced toward Harris's encampment on the Salt River and his first battle as a commander. He was nervous, but when he reached the enemy campsite in a dry creek bottom, he found that the Missouri guerrillas had fled. Grant realized that Harris had been as afraid of him as he had been of Harris. He later confessed, "This was a view of the question I had never taken before; but it was one I never forgot afterward." In all of his future battles, he never panicked and faced his enemies with a calmness.

On the last day of July 1861, Grant received word that he had been promoted to brigadier general, with his new rank backdated to May 17. The chaplain of the 21st Illinois had stumbled across the news in a copy of the *Missouri Daily Democrat* and had rushed to Grant's tent to tell him. The new general, though pleased to hear the news, replied, "Well, sir, I had no suspicion of it. . . . That's some of Washburne's work." The congressman who had recommended him to Governor Yates had also recommended him to receive one of four appointments for general allotted to the state of Illinois.

A few days later, Grant was ordered to move his regiment to Ironton, seventy miles south of St. Louis, and to assume command of the District of Southeast Missouri, which included southern Illinois and was headquartered in Cairo. He served briefly in Ironton,

Cairo, Illinois, 1861. At the center of this photograph, Grant and fellow commander John McClernand await the arrival of their uniforms at the Cairo post office.

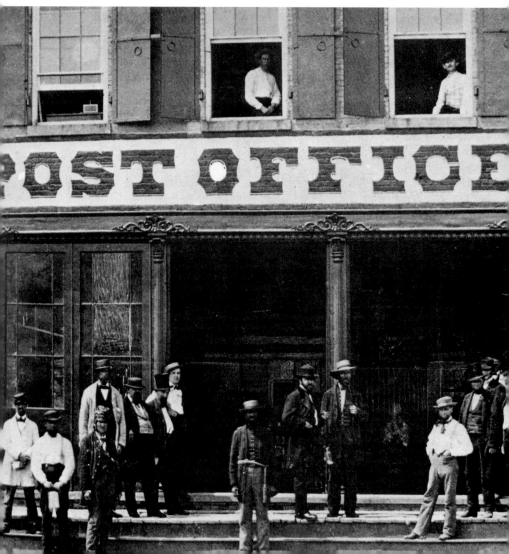

Jefferson City, and Cape Girardeau, fortifying those locations against possible attack by Missouri guerrillas, then moved to Cairo, Illinois, to establish his command post on September 4.

The western theater of the Civil War was very different from the conflict in the east. With the exception of a few battles, most of the major battles in the east, at least until late in 1864 when Sherman marched north through Georgia and the Carolinas, would be concentrated in a

This 1862 map shows the heart of the war's western theater, marking battlefields, forts, state boundaries, railroads, and towns. *(Library of Congress)*

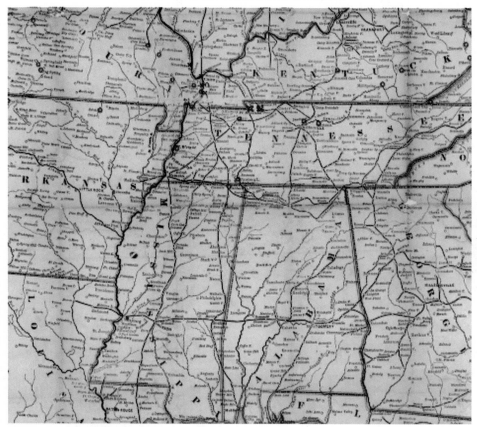

relatively small area between Washington, D. C., and the Confederate capital at Richmond, Virginia. In the west, vast amounts of terrain were covered and the focus was on securing and maintaining tactically important locations. It was important to both sides to try to get control of—and the support of—the border states. The Union wanted to contain and then slowly constrict the Confederates, while the Confederates wanted to defend as much land as they could.

Grant's timely move to Cairo put him in perfect position to confront an enemy incursion into Kentucky that had begun a day earlier when Confederate Major General Leonidas Polk ordered Brigadier General Gideon J. Pillow to seize and fortify the heights of Columbus, Kentucky. Polk, a West Point classmate of Jefferson Davis, had left the army to become an Episcopal bishop in Louisiana, but had returned to military service at the outbreak of hostilities. Columbus was the terminus for the Mobile and Ohio Railroad, and occupied a commanding location on the Mississippi River across from Belmont, Missouri. Polk recognized the strategic importance of the town and moved first to secure it.

Grant countered Polk's action with a move against Paducah, Kentucky, about forty-five miles northeast of Cairo on the Ohio River. Paducah controlled the mouths of the Tennessee and Cumberland rivers, waterways that led deep into the heart of the Confederacy. Without waiting for authorization from General Frémont, Grant loaded a force of fifteen hundred Union soldiers and four artillery pieces aboard three riverboats, steamed up the Ohio River, and occupied the town on September 6. He issued a proclamation at once, stating, in part: "The strong arm of the Government is here to protect its friends, and to punish only its enemies."

Grant's decisive action effectively forestalled a Confederate effort to seize the mouth of the Tennessee River and was decisive in keeping Kentucky in the Union. Four days after Grant occupied Paducah, Confederate President Jefferson Davis gave General Albert S. Johnston, one of the most gifted of his officers, command of all Confederate armies in the West.

Meanwhile, in Washington, D.C., the aging and ill Lieutenant General Winfield Scott resigned as the army's general in chief on the first day of November. He was replaced later in the month by Major General George B. McClellan. Scott left behind a strategy for winning the war that recognized it would take time to raise, train, and equip an army large enough to defeat the South. In the interim, he called for blockading the seacoast and sealing off the inland borders. When the North became strong enough, it would first move down the Mississippi and constrict the Confederacy, after which it would send armies of superior force into the South to destroy the outnumbered Confederate forces. When news of Scott's plan leaked out, journalists labeled it the "Anaconda Plan" and derided it as being far too slow for any use. They considered it to be an old man's plan; in the first months, both sides anticipated a quick war. As events played out, however, Scott's plan was very close to the strategy actually employed by the North.

In another surprise, Lincoln relieved General Fremont of his command the day after Scott resigned, and named Major General Henry W. Halleck as his replacement. Halleck took command of the Western Department—now renamed the Department of Missouri—on November 19. Grant now reported to Halleck, who was an excellent military theoretician and administrator, but a less effective field commander.

On November 7, 1861, Grant led a contingent of 3,114 troops in transports twelve miles down the Mississippi River from Cairo and attacked a Confederate camp held by troops of Major General Sterling Price's command. Advancing through the woods, Grant's men drove Price's troops to the river's edge in four hours of savage fighting.

Then the Union troops, prematurely elated at what they thought was a victory, halted their celebration when Polk sent ten thousand reinforcements across the river from Columbus, hoping to cut Grant's troops off from their transports. Grant described the situation later: "The alarm 'surrounded' was given. . . . At first some of the officers seemed to think that to be surrounded was to be placed in a hopeless position, where there was nothing to do but surrender. But when I announced that we had cut our way in and could cut our way out just as well, it seemed a new revelation to officers and soldiers."

Grant and his soldiers proceeded to cut their way out of an encirclement and made it back to their transport successfully, after inflicting more than six hundred Confederate casualties and taking about as many of its own. Grant's foray fell short of a stunning victory, but he was just getting started. Moreover, at a time when the Union was suffering early defeats in both the East and the West, he was demonstrating a willingness to strike his foes with whatever resources at his disposal.

At the start of 1862, the strategic importance of the river routes into the South became the focus in the West. The Confederate strongpoint at Columbus, with its heavy guns and garrison of twenty thousand men, effectively blocked off the Mississippi. General Sidney Johnston knew that a Federal invasion was coming and that it would surely follow the routes of the Cumberland River, which led to Nashville, and the Tennessee River, which coursed all the way to Mississippi and Alabama. Just below the Kentucky line, Johnston had built two forts to attempt to block Union progress up the two rivers—Fort Henry on the Tennessee and Fort Donelson on the Cumberland.

In late January, Grant sent a telegram to General Halleck: "With permission I will take Fort Henry on the Tennessee and hold and establish a large camp there." On January 30, 1862, Halleck informed Grant that Fort Henry was to be "taken and held at all hazards."

From February 2 to 5, Grant ferried a force of about fifteen thousand men in transports to within four miles

Foote's intimidating gunboat floatilla attacks Fort Henry from the Tennessee River.

of Fort Henry. Acting in concert with Grant's forces, a squadron of seven new ironclad gunboats, commanded by Commodore Andrew H. Foote, steamed up the Tennessee River and began firing on the fort in preparation for a land attack by Grant's troops. Fort Henry proved less formidable than Grant or Foote had anticipated. Confederate Brigadier General Lloyd Tilghman, recognizing the fort's vulnerability—it had been built on low ground and was already partly under water from the rising Tennessee, which was approaching flood stage— had already evacuated twenty-five hundred men to Fort Donelson, eleven miles to the east. The seventy-nine remaining artillerymen returned fire from Foote's gunboats only briefly before surrendering. Before Grant's men could position themselves for attack, the fight was over. The siege cost Foote less than one hundred men, against about the same number of Confederate casualties.

Grant, spoiling for action, reported to Halleck: "I shall take and destroy Fort Donelson on the 8th and

This historic map shows the layout of Fort Donelson along the banks of the Cumberland River. As a result of Foote's support from the river, Grant was able to lauch a successful land attack from the east.

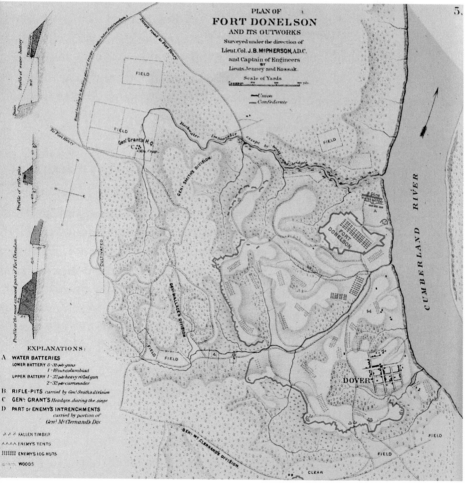

return to Fort Henry." This time he did not ask his superior's permission. Foote returned to the Ohio River with his flotilla and then entered the Cumberland River to lend support for Grant's overland assault. Heavy rains and flooding delayed Grant's attack for a week, however, during which time General Johnston reinforced Fort Donelson to bring its garrison strength to about twenty thousand troops. Unlike Fort Henry, Fort Donelson was prepared for a fight.

On February 12, Grant marched eastward and besieged Fort Donelson. The main Union elements consisted of the 1st, 2nd, and 3rd Divisions, commanded by Brigadier Generals John A. McClernand, Charles F. Smith, and Lew Wallace, respectively. While waiting for all of his forces to arrive, Grant probed the fort's defenses on February 13. The next day, Commodore Foote and six gunboats of his western flotilla moved upriver in an effort to pummel the fort into submission as he had at Fort Henry, but well-positioned Confederate guns drove them away. Foote was severely wounded.

Overall command of the Confederate defense of Fort Donelson resided with Brigadier General John B. Floyd; Brigadier General Gideon J. Pillow was second in command; and Brigadier General Simon Bolivar Buckner, Grant's old friend, was third in command. Grant held both Floyd and Pillow in low esteem. "Floyd . . . who was a man of talent enough for any civil position, was no soldier," he wrote after the war, and he later told Buckner that had he captured Pillow at Fort Donelson, he would

Grant, astride his favorite stallion, Jack, inspects the fighting at Fort Donelson from a nearby rise.

have set him free. "I would rather have him in command of you fellows than as a prisoner," Grant explained. Of the three commanders, Grant respected only Buckner as a soldier.

The Confederate commanders trapped in the besieged fort recognized the hopelessness of their situation. On February 15, they tried to fight their way out. Initially, with Pillow's forces leading the assault, their attack beat the Federal forces back. Then, Grant rode out to check on his troops. When he noticed the full packs on some of the enemy dead, he surmised that the Confederates were trying to escape. Grant spread the word among his men at once: "Whichever party makes the first attack will win the day, and the rebels will have to be very quick to beat me." He ordered Smith to attack, with Foote and Wallace offering whatever support they could. Pillow made the critical mistake of ordering his troops back to the fort where they were pinned down and defeated.

That night, Floyd passed his command to Pillow, who promptly turned it over to Buckner. During the night, Floyd and Pillow escaped by boat, leaving the distasteful task of surrendering the fort to their third in command. Some fifteen hundred Confederates escaped with them, and Colonel Nathan Bedford Forrest led his seven hun-

Grant's West Point friend, Confederate general S. B. Buckner. *(Library of Congress)*

dred cavalry troopers across icy backwaters to safety. Buckner, who also might have chosen to escape, felt duty bound to stay and suffer the indignity of surrender along with his troops. In the middle of the night, he sent a message to Grant requesting surrender terms. Grant replied: "No terms except unconditional and immediate surrender can be accepted. I propose to move immediately upon your works." Buckner considered Grant's terms unduly harsh, but he had no choice but to accept them.

On February 16, between twelve thousand and fifteen thousand Confederates surrendered to Grant. In addition, great quantities of arms and ammunition, artillery, horses, and commissary stores passed into Federal hands. Grant's victory cost him almost three thousand men. Shortly after Buckner surrendered, Grant pulled him aside. Remembering his old friend's kindness to him during a rough period in his own life, Grant said, "Buckner, you are, I know, separated from your people, and perhaps you need funds; my purse is at your disposal." Buckner thanked him for his kindness but graciously declined.

After Grant's twin victories the Confederate garrison at Columbus was forced to pull out. There was a Union army under General Don Carlos Buell heading toward Nashville from the north, and another force was aligning against Columbus from across the Mississippi. General Johnston had no choice but to order his armies out of the two cities, which left all of Kentucky and most of Tennessee in Federal control. Poor leadership, violation of the military principle of unity of command, and an inflexible defensive stance had cost the Confederacy control of the two strategically critical forts. In the North, news of these still rare Union victories brought Grant his first taste of national publicity. He was, almost inevitably, dubbed "Unconditional Surrender" Grant.

Lincoln's Man

In Washington, President Lincoln ordered a promotion for Grant. On February 20, 1862, the *Chicago Tribune* reported: "Gen. Ulysses S. Grant, the hero of Fort Donelson, has just been unanimously confirmed by the Senate as Major General [of volunteers], an honor conferred in testimony of his gallant conduct in battle." The day after the fall of Fort Donelson, Grant's command was renamed the District of West Tennessee. Eventually it would expand into the Department and Army of the Tennessee. General Halleck installed General William Tecumseh Sherman in Grant's old headquarters in Cairo. In another month, Grant would rank as the senior subordinate commander under Halleck.

Grant had suggested attacking Nashville immediately after Fort Donelson fell. He knew it was a strategic target and vulnerable. Halleck restrained him, however, by explaining that Nashville was in Major General Don Carlos Buell's command sector. In the meantime, a division of troops from Buell's Army of the Ohio had been sent to reinforce Grant's assault on Donelson. When the division arrived a week late, Grant, without consulting either Halleck or Buell, sent the late arrivals back to Buell, who was approaching Nashville. Grant did not know that the Confederates had left the Tennessee capital.

Nashville was occupied without a fight on February 26. Soon after, Grant made a visit to the city. Halleck, who was beginning to be concerned by Grant's rapid rise to prominence, complained to General George McClellan that Grant had a habit of failing to inform him of his situation and future plans. Halleck even hinted that Grant had left his command behind in

Major General Henry Halleck. *(Library of Congress)*

order to visit Nashville to resume his old drinking habits. "It is hard to censure a successful general," Halleck told McClellan, "but I think he richly deserves it."

McClellan, who had met Grant briefly at Fort Vancouver at the nadir of Grant's career, also assumed that he was still drinking heavily. "Do not hesitate to arrest him at once if the good of the service requires it and place C. F. Smith in command," McClellan answered Halleck. "You are at liberty to regard this as a positive order." Halleck accepted McClellan's order and replaced Grant—however unjustly—with C. F. Smith, who had been Grant's commanding officer at West Point.

While it is possible that Grant was drinking while in Nashville, he had not been remiss in maintaining communication with Halleck. A later investigation revealed that a Confederate sympathizer in the telegraph office was preventing Grant's messages from reaching Halleck in St. Louis. Halleck, realizing the absurdity of arresting Grant—a fighting general at the height of his acclaim—relented and reinstated him on March 11. But Halleck had succeeded in damaging Grant's reputation. Also on March 11, President Lincoln named Halleck the supreme commander in the West; he controlled all Unioin forces from the Appalachian Mountains to the Mississippi River. As Grant's commander, Halleck would receive much of the credit for his subordinate's victories at Forts Henry and Donelson, while rumors of Grant's drinking, so skillfully magnified by Halleck, would taint his reputation and slow his advancement over the next two years.

Halleck's new position gave him control of four armies—Buell's Army of the Ohio, Grant's Army of the Tennessee, Major General Samuel R. Curtis's Army of the Southwest in Missouri and Arkansas, and Major General John Pope's Army of the Mississippi. Halleck—or "Old Brains," as he had become known for his intellectual skills as a military theoretician—decided the next step was to move against Sidney Johnston's Confederate forces at Corinth, Mississippi. The two armies of Grant and Buell were sent to Pittsburg Landing, Tennessee.

On March 17, 1862, Grant returned to his command from Nashville. His army had grown from the three divisions he commanded at Fort Donelson to six. Five divisions were concentrated at Pittsburg Landing on the west bank of the Tennessee River, and a sixth was being formed from the reinforcements that were arriving daily. The new 4th, 5th, and 6th Divisions were led by Brigadier Generals Stephen A. Hurlbut, William T. Sherman, and Benjamin M. Prentiss, respectively. Grant established his headquarters at Savannah, Tennessee, eight miles downstream from the Union encampment at Pittsburg Landing, and prepared to march on Corinth, twenty miles southwest of Pittsburg Landing, as soon as General Buell's Army of the Ohio arrived from Nashville. Because Grant planned to take the initiative, and their encampment was to be only temporary, neither he nor his subordinate commanders took steps to fortify their positions. As Grant later explained, they "had no expectation of needing fortifications, though this subject was taken into consideration." He saw no reason to have his men dig in when he planned a fast-moving strike against Cornith. This decision to not fortify would later become highly controversial.

In Corinth, General Johnston was aware of the Union movements and the impending threat. He decided that his best option was to attack Grant quickly, before Buell arrived from Nashville. Johnston marched north out of Corinth on the afternoon of April 3 with forty thousand men. His progress was slowed by roads muddied by the spring rains and lack of discipline of his unruly, green troops shooting at rabbits and deer along the way. It took two days to travel the twenty-two miles; they arrived on the night of April 5. Unaware that an equally large Confederate army was camped just two miles away, Grant's forces slept without a care that night.

Grant was in a highly vulnerable position. His encampment was pocketed by a creek on each side and the Tennessee River at its back, and was virtually surrounded by higher ground. Most of the camp was concentrated around a country meeting house known as Shiloh Church.

In the Confederate camp, in the dark before dawn, General Johnston primed his troops for battle by telling them the "eyes and hopes of eight millions of people rest upon you." Johnston then commenced his attack at dawn on April 6. His gray-clad troops burst out of the surrounding woods and took the Federals by complete surprise. The battle of Shiloh (April 6–7, 1862)—or

Pittsburg Landing, as it was known to Northerners—exploded across the quiet Tennessee countryside.

In the first day's fighting, the Confederates almost drove Grant's army into the Tennessee River, but Union resistance finally organized at the "Hornets' Nest" (so called because of the stinging shot and shell faced by the attackers), a partially eroded wagon trace that formed a natural defensive position. This delayed the Confederate attack and wreaked havoc on Johnston's timetable. Then, at about 2:30 PM, Johnston took a bullet in the leg that severed an artery; he bled to death in minutes. General Pierre G. T. Beauregard, Johnston's second in command, took over and managed to press the Union

The Union army was able to hold off Johnston's forces on the first day of the battle of Shiloh by organizing their lines along the densely wooded Hornet's Nest. *(Library of Congress)*

troops to their last defense line in front of Pittsburg Landing by nightfall.

The Confederates had scored a victory in the first day, but at a terrible price. Their talented commander was dead, and by dark many of the soldiers were totally exhausted and disorganized and some units were dangerously low on ammunition. Although Beauregard did not know it, his narrow window of opportunity to attack before the arrival of some twenty-five thousand Union reinforcements was rapidly closing. The first divisions of Buell's army had already arrived; the remainder would be there by morning. Like most of the other officers, he thought the Yankees were whipped. He thought it was best to not attack the landing that night, but to reorganize and rest and finish off Grant's trapped army the next morning.

That night, a soft drizzle began to fall at about ten o'clock. Grant sat with his staff around a fire. After an inspection tour, Colonel James B. McPherson, the senior engineering officer, reported that a third of the army had been knocked out of action and the rest were downcast and dejected. Given the situation, McPherson asked, "Shall I make preparations for retreat?"

Grant looked at him with amazement. "Retreat?" he asked. "No. I propose to attack at daylight and whip them."

At dawn, Grant, now reinforced by Buell's army, sent his troops forward and recaptured all that had been lost the day before. By mid-afternoon, it was clear that the Confederate army was outnumbered and exhausted.

Grant leads his troops into battle at dawn on the second day of Shiloh. *(Library of Congress)*

One of Beauregard's aides asked, "General, do you not think our troops are in the condition of a lump of sugar thoroughly soaked with water, but yet preserving its original shape, though ready to dissolve?" Beauregard thought they were, and he began his retreat to Corinth.

Grant did not give chase. His own army was fought out, too. He later summed up the battle this way:

> Shiloh was the severest battle fought at the West during the war, and but few in the East equalled it for hard, determined fighting. . . . The result was a Union victory that gave the men who achieved it great confidence in themselves ever after. . . . The Confederates fought with courage at Shiloh. . . . It is possible that the Southern man started with a little more dash than his Northern brother; but he was correspondingly less enduring.

The narrow Union victory cost Grant more than thirteen thousand men. His adversary reported more than ten thousand killed, wounded, or missing. Of the roughly one hundred thousand men who fought at Shiloh, almost one out of every four was killed.

In failing to destroy Grant's army at the battle of Shiloh, which was at the time the bloodiest battle ever fought on the North American continent, the South failed in its last, best bid to regain western Tennessee. It was the point of no return for Confederate fortunes in the West. That same month, Union General Samuel Curtis's army defeated Brigadier General Earl Van Dorn's Confederate army at Pea Ridge, Arkansas, and John Pope's won decisive Federal victories at New Madrid and Island No. 10 on the Mississippi River. Farther south, Vice Admiral David G. Farragut's West Gulf Blockading Squadron blasted its way through Confederate Forts Jackson and St. Philip, which bracketed the Mississippi almost fifty miles south of New Orleans, and seized the strategic Mississippi port by month's end.

After Shiloh, Grant was—at first—again hailed as a great hero. When the fearsome casualty counts and reports of Union unpreparedness became known, however, public sentiment turned against him. His detractors called him a heartless butcher who covered his own mistakes with the blood of his men. Once again, rumors began to circulate that Grant was a drunk and that was why he had been taken by surprise. He became an easy scapegoat for an uneasy public, trying to understand the slaughter that consumed their country. He had one very important ally, however. President Lincoln put a stop to demands for Grant's removal with a characteristically pithy comment: "I can't spare this man; he fights."

On April 11, General Halleck arrived at Pittsburg Landing to assume direct command of the Union forces gathering for an advance on Corinth, including Grant's Army of the Tennessee, Buell's Army of the Ohio, and Pope's Army of the Mississippi. Halleck, still wary of Grant's rising favor in high places, "elevated" Grant to second in command, a position without much responsibility that was calculated to limit the possibility of him enhancing his reputation. As a result, Grant played little role in Halleck's cautious, month-long advance on Corinth.

By the time Halleck's forces reached Corinth on May 30, Beauregard had already evacuated and the Federals occupied the city without opposition. Grant later wrote, "For myself I was little more than an observer. . . . My position was so embarrassing in fact that I made several applications during the siege to be relieved." His applications were denied. Grant went on to note, "I am satisfied that Corinth could have been captured in a two days' campaign commenced promptly on the arrival of reinforcements after the battle of Shiloh." He believed strongly that a quicker campaign would have at least partially destroyed Beauregard's army, which would have meant fewer foes to face on a later day.

Throughout June, Confederate positions continued

to fall. General Beauregard withdrew his army to a new line along the Tuscumbia River in Alabama, which left Fort Pillow on the Mississippi vulnerable. The Confederates evacuated the fort on June 4. Two days later, following a naval battle and bombardment, Union forces occupied Memphis, Tennessee. Only a 200-mile stretch of the mighty Mississippi River, between Vicksburg, Mississippi, and Port Hudson, Louisiana, remained under Confederate control. Moreover, the fall of Memphis delivered control of four key rail lines to the Union.

On July 11, 1862, President Lincoln recalled General Halleck to Washington and appointed him general in chief of all the Union armies. Grant resumed command of the District of West Tennessee, with the defensive mission of safeguarding Union conquests from Paducah to Corinth, including Memphis. "During the two months after the departure of General Halleck there was much fighting between small bodies of the contending armies," Grant recalled years later, "but these encounters were dwarfed by the magnitude of the main battles so as to be now almost forgotten except by those engaged in them." The clash of troops at Iuka, in the northeast corner of Mississippi, was typical of those "almost forgotten" encounters in the summer and early fall of 1862.

On September 13, Confederate General Sterling Price shifted his army of fourteen thousand troops from Tupelo, Mississippi, to Iuka. Price's presence threatened Grant's communication with Buell's army in eastern Tennessee. Grant sent Major General Edward O. C. Ord eastward with eight thousand troops to engage Price, while Major General William S. Rosecrans circled swiftly to the south with nine thousand men to cut off Price's expected withdrawal. "It looked to me," Grant noted later, "that if Price would remain in Iuka until we got there, his

Major General William S. Rosecrans. *(Library of Congress)*

annihilation was inevitable." When Rosecrans approached within two miles of Iuka on September 19, however, Price's left flank suddenly struck the Federals and a fierce two-hour battle broke out.

"The fight began," Price reported later, "and was waged with a severity I have never seen surpassed." In the inconclusive encounter, Grant's casualties numbered over seven hundred, Price's over fifteen hundred. When Price heard that Ord was preparing to join the fight the next day, he gathered his forces and slipped away in the night. Two weeks later, Price and Earl Van Dorn struck Rosecrans again at Corinth. The Union forces saved the city, but the Confederates again eluded Grant's attempt to destroy them.

In late 1862, Grant, from his headquarters in Holly Springs, Mississippi, began to focus on clearing the last Confederate strongpoint on the Mississippi River at Vicksburg. The Confederates repulsed the first attempt to breach Vicksburg's defenses at Chickasaw Bluffs at the end of 1862. On the first day of 1863, President Lincoln issued the Emancipation Proclamation, which freed the slaves of the secessionist states. Although his edict could not yet be consistently enforced in the South, it established a clear moral goal for the war and discouraged European countries from lending support to the Confederacy.

Meanwhile, fighting in the eastern theater was intense but unproductive. Most of the battles were concentrated in a bloody crucible between the two capitals—Washington in the North and Richmond in the South—and neither side could gain a definitive advantage.

During the first three months of 1863, Grant launched four more unsuccessful attempts to seize or isolate the town of Vicksburg—by way of, in turn, the Lake Providence route, a canal bypassing the city, the Steele's Bayou route, and the Yazoo Pass route. Grant next planned a wide envelopment of the city from the south and east.

Despite Grant's five failed attempts to capture Vicksburg, President Lincoln continued to support him. To an advisor who suggested replacing Grant, Lincoln said, "I rather like the man; I think we'll try him a little longer." In the spring of 1863, Grant led his Army of the

This map of Vicksburg and the surrounding area, made in 1863, shows the town's challenging position along the Mississippi River. *(Library of Congress)*

Tennessee down the west bank of the Mississippi, determined to once and for all dislodge the Vicksburg garrison of some thirty thousand troops under the command of Confederate Lieutenant General John C. Pemberton. In a patient, methodical campaign carried out in several phases, Grant justified the president's faith in him.

On the night of April 16, Rear Admiral David D. Porter, the local Union naval commander, led his flotilla of gunboats and transports towing barges past the formidable Confederate batteries at Vicksburg to a landing site called Hard Times, twenty-eight miles to the south. The next night, to divert attention from his movements, Grant sent three cavalry regiments totaling seventeen hundred men under Colonel Benjamin Grierson on an extended raid of some six hundred miles. The raiders started at La Grange, Tennessee, swept through Mississippi, and arrived at Baton Rouge, Louisiana, on May 2. Along the way they cut Confederate railway and tele-

This lithograph print depicts the night of April 16, 1863 when Admiral Porter's fleet ran the Confederate blockade of the Mississippi at Vicksburg. *(Library of Congress)*

graph lines, and effectively isolated the Mississippi
state capital of Jackson.

On April 30, Admiral Porter's transports ferried two
of Grant's corps—Major General John A. McClernand's
13 Corps, and Major General James B. McPherson's 17
Corps—across the river to Bruinsburg, nine miles south
of Hard Times. He had left Sherman's 15 Corps at the
Yazoo River northwest of the city to divert Confederate
attention from the crossing. His other two corps met no
opposition on the east bank and fanned out rapidly into
hostile territory. They carried only enough rations for
five days and did not have a clear line of supply or
retreat. Grant had told Sherman earlier that the Union
troops would carry only "what rations of hard bread,
coffee, and salt we can and make the country furnish the
balance." Sherman considered Grant's projected campaign too risky, but dutifully carried out his orders.

Early in Grant's Vicksburg campaign, the Confederates were hampered by a split command. President
Jefferson Davis had sent General Joseph E. Johnston, a
smart, feisty, and aggressive commander, to Jackson,
Mississippi, to assume overall Confederate command in
the West. Johnston's task entailed coordinating two
separated armies: General John C. Pemberton's in Mississippi and General Braxton Bragg's in Tennessee. Davis
further complicated Johnston's difficult situation by
ordering Pemberton to defend Vicksburg at all costs.
Johnston saw Vicksburg as a potential trap and ordered
Pemberton to move against Grant. Pemberton was in an

impossible situation. He needed to keep Vicksburg to keep the Mississippi open, but he had other territory to defend, and not enough troops to do either. In an effort to serve two masters, he strung out his forces from Vicksburg to Jackson. By so doing, he failed to uphold the cardinal military dictate to concentrate his forces. Grant took full advantage of Pemberton's quandary and sliced between his army and Johnston's force of about six thousand in Jackson.

Grant wrested Port Gibson from Brigadier General John S. Bowen's Confederate defenders after some hard fighting and established a beachhead. Grant next decided to neutralize Johnston's army before turning on Vicksburg. On May 13, he marched on Jackson with Sherman—now reunited with Grant's army—and McPherson leading the assault; McClernand trailed behind to hold off Pemberton, if necessary. Under attack, Johnston chose to abandon Jackson and Federal troops marched into the Mississippi capital the next day. Sherman stayed there to occupy the city and protect against a possible counterattack by Johnston; Grant turned to engage Pemberton's advancing forces.

On May 16, as Grant moved westward toward Vicksburg with a force of twenty-nine thousand, Pemberton met him with an army of twenty-two thousand. A major battle erupted at Champion's Hill. Grant forced Pemberton to withdraw, and the next day Pemberton engaged in another costly encounter with Grant at the Big Black River. Pemberton then turned and

In one of Grant's most resolute moves of the war, Union troops laid siege to the city of Vicksburg from May 18 to July 4, 1863. *(Library of Congress)*

rushed back to Vicksburg with Grant in close pursuit.

Grant arrived at Vicksburg on May 18. By then, his army had covered 200 miles and had won four major battles. He mounted two major assaults on the city (May 18 and 22) at great cost and to no avail. Describing the attacks, Sherman noted, "The heads of columns have been swept away as chaff from the hands on a windy day." Grant paused to rethink his strategy.

"I now determined upon a regular siege—to 'out-camp the enemy,' as it were, and to incur no more losses," he wrote later. "The experience of the 22d [in which he sustained more than three thousand casualties] convinced officers and men that this was best, and they went to work on the defences [sic] and approaches with a will." Grant and his forces settled in to a traditional siege posture and allowed shelling, hunger, and disease to erode the enemy's will to resist.

By July 1, Vicksburg's defenders and civilians had been reduced to eating horses and mules. Grant's forces had advanced their position for another assault. Facing certain defeat, Pemberton surrendered the city on July 4, 1863. By odd coincidence, Grant's great victory at

Ulysses S. Grant in 1863, shortly after his promotion to major general. *(Library of Congress)*

Vicksburg came on the same day of Confederate General Robert E. Lee's retreat from the battlefield at Gettysburg, Pennsylvania. Within two days, the last attempt by Lee to take the war to the north had been soundly defeated and the last Confederate stronghold on the vital Mississippi River had fallen.

The fall of Vicksburg, and the capture of Port Hudson downstream five days later, opened the entire Mississippi to the Union. In Washington, Lincoln said, "The Father of Waters again goes unvexed to the sea." The Confederacy was finally split in half and could no longer draw on the flow of replacements, horses, cattle, pigs, sugar, and salt from Arkansas, Louisiana, and Texas.

Grant's victory earned him Lincoln's unshakable confidence. He was promoted to the rank of major general in the Regular Army, effective July 4, 1863. Of Grant, the president said: "He doesn't worry and bother me. He isn't shrieking for reinforcements all the time. He takes what troops we can safely give him . . . and does the best he can with what he has got. And if Grant only does this thing right down there . . . why, Grant is my man and I am his the rest of the war."

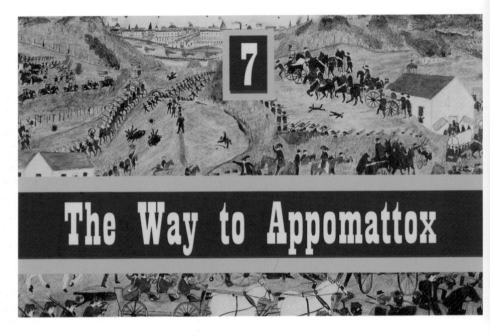

The Way to Appomattox

After the fall of Vicksburg and Port Hudson, Grant sent Sherman back to Jackson to drive Johnston's army out of Mississippi. As Sherman quickly accomplished this task, Grant sustained a serious injury when a new, spirited horse fell with its full weight on his hip and leg, and it took three months to heal.

Meanwhile, in Tennessee, Major General William S. Rosecrans's Union Army of the Cumberland advanced on Chattanooga and drove Major General Braxton Bragg's Confederate Army of Tennessee into Georgia. Rosecrans entered the city on September 9, 1863, but, in attempting to pursue Bragg, his own forces became dispersed over a forty-mile front. On September 19, Bragg, reinforced by a corps under James Longstreet, counterattacked Rosecrans near Chickamauga Creek in

Thomas's Union line advances through dense forest toward Longstreet's forces at Chickamauga. *(Library of Congress)*

northwest Georgia. The next day, Longstreet attacked again and pierced the Union lines. The day was saved for the North when Major General George H. Thomas and his U.S. 16th Infantry held off the Confederate attack long enough for Rosecrans and most of his army to make it back to Chattanooga. For this feat Thomas earned the nickname "Rock of Chickamauga."

That afternoon, as one Confederate soldier described, "the dead were piled upon each other in ricks [stacks], like cord wood, to make passage for advancing columns. The sluggish Chickamauga ran red with human blood." Federal losses totaled over sixteen thousand; Confederate casualties numbered nearly twelve thousand. The

newly emboldened Bragg established positions on Lookout Mountain and Missionary Ridge and began a Confederate siege of Chattanooga.

In October, U.S. Secretary of War Edwin McMasters
Stanton combined the three departments of the Ohio, the
Cumberland, and the Tennessee into one command named
the Military Division of the Mississippi, and placed
Grant at its head. Grant assumed the new command in
Louisville, Kentucky, on October 18, 1863. He immediately ordered Rosecrans—whom President Lincoln said
"acted like a duck hit in the head" after Chickamauga—
to turn over command of his army to Thomas. A few days
later, on October 23, Grant moved to break Bragg's siege
of Chattanooga.

Grant struck Bragg with the full force of the fifty-six
thousand troops available to him—two corps of
Sherman's Army of the Tennessee, two corps of the Army
of the Potomac under Major General Joseph Hooker, and
Thomas's Army of the Cumberland. Bragg fielded sixty-
four thousand troops. The battle of Chattanooga (November 23–27, 1863)—also known as the battle of
Missionary Ridge—was fought precisely as Grant recalled it years later: "Sherman was to get on Missionary
Ridge, as he did; Hooker to cross the north end of
Lookout Mountain, as he did, sweep across Chattanooga
Valley and get across the south end of the ridge near
Rossville." At that point, Thomas assaulted Bragg's center,
and Grant broke the siege on the city, forcing Bragg to
withdraw again into northern Georgia. Grant, in a letter

On November 23-24, Grant's forces captured Orchard Knob and Lookout Mountain, shown here on the horizon. On November 25, Union soldiers broke through the seemingly impenetrable Confederate position on Missionary Ridge, and at last the Union held Chattanooga, the "Gateway to the Lower South," which became the supply and logistics base for Sherman's 1864 Atlanta Campaign. *(Library of Congress)*

to his beloved Julia, told her of "the utter rout and demoralization of the enemy."

Two days later, on November 29, Confederate General Longstreet, who had detached from Bragg with ten thousand infantry and five thousand cavalry, attacked Knoxville, Tennessee, in the eastern part of the state. The city was being held by the Union Army of the Ohio under its new commander, Major General Ambrose E. Burnside. Grant sent Sherman to Burnside's aid and saved Knoxville. On December 8, 1863, the *New York Tribune* reported: "The siege of Knoxville is at an end. The Rebel effort to regain East Tennessee is abandoned forever."

Following Grant's extraordinary string of tactical

victories that yielded great strategic advantage to the
Union—Forts Henry and Donelson, Shiloh, Vicksburg,
Chattanooga, and Knoxville—talk of him being a presidential candidate began to circulate in Washington.
Grant assured President Lincoln that he held no such
ambitions. "My son," the president told him, "you will
never know how gratifying that is to me."

On March 10, 1864, Lincoln promoted him to lieu-

The certificate appointing Grant lieutenant general of the Union forces.

tenant general, effective March 2. Grant became the first American officer to hold this top rank since George Washington. Grant now supplanted his old boss Halleck as general in chief of all the Federal armies. Grant, always the battlefield officer, intended, unlike Halleck, to make his "headquarters [with] armies in the field."

Grant was now responsible for the entire Union war effort. Finally, he was going to focus most of his efforts in the eastern front and begin the final battle with the legendary Confederate General Robert E. Lee and his Army of Northern Virginia.

There were first some organizational changes to be made. When Grant took overall command of the Union armies, as he wrote later, "There were . . . seventeen distinct commanders. Before this time these various armies had acted separately and independently of each other, giving the enemy an opportunity often of depleting one command, not pressed, to reinforce another more actively engaged. I determined to stop this."

To attack Lee in Virginia, the heart of Confederate power, Grant devised a two-fold approach. First, in terms of strategy, he explained: "My general plan now was to concentrate all the force possible against the Confederate armies in the field. . . . Accordingly, I arranged for a simultaneous movement all along the line."

Grant viewed his different armies as unified parts of a single, larger whole—a grand army with himself as supreme commander. Previous Union strategies had employed armies as separate entities operating indepen-

This photograph of Grant was taken in the spring of 1864, just after Lincoln promoted him to lieutenant general. *(Library of Congress)*

dently of one another, which had enabled the Confederates to shift their forces to aid others more endangered. Grant's vision of one irresistible force applying simultaneous pressure on his enemy everywhere was calculated to take full advantage of the North's superiority in manpower and materials. Confederates fully engaged everywhere at once would no longer shift forces. Union conquests outside Virginia, for example, would gradually reduce the sources of General Lee's manpower and vital resources.

Grant aimed the second part of his two-fold strategy at defeating Lee directly. "Lee, with the capital of the Confederacy, was the main end to which all were working," Grant noted later. On May 4, 1864, he stationed himself in central Virginia and launched his "grand campaign," which was designed not to occupy territory, as previous Union efforts in the east had often been, but to destroy the two remaining Confederate armies—Lee's Army of Northern Virginia and a consolidated Western army under Joseph Johnston. To this end, Grant sent General George Meade, commander of the Army of the Potomac, across the Rapidan River to move toward Richmond, the Confederate capital. "Lee's army will be your objective point," Grant told Meade. "Wherever Lee goes, there you will go also."

Simultaneously, Grant sent Major General Phillip Sheridan into the Shenandoah Valley to ravage Confederate supply sources, and ordered Sherman, who had replaced him as commander of the Union forces in the

West, to march into Georgia after Joseph Johnston. Grant's written order to Sherman said, in part: "You I propose to move against Johnston's army, to break it up and to get into the interior of the enemy's country as far as you can, inflicting all the damage you can against their war resources." Grant advocated a war waged with complete conviction and absolute commitment of national resources to destroy an enemy's ability to reciprocate. He thought this was the best way to bring the brutal conflict to a final close.

Although Grant exercised control of all the Union armies, he detached himself to Meade's Army of the Potomac and remained in the east for the rest of the war. He left the tactics of warfare—the art of maneuvering or placing troops in battle—to his subordinate commanders. Matters of strategy—the planning and directing of an entire war or campaign—he reserved for himself. These questions involved such things as deciding whether an attack should be made, and where and when it should happen; who should command; how manpower and resources should be allocated; and how best to use lines of communication and transportation— telegraph, railways, waterways, and so on. The success of his operations could often be attributed to his expert knowledge of logistics, which he had learned as a quartermaster in Mexico and applied on the Mississippi River in combined naval-land operations.

As Grant planned and prepared for his grand campaign in early 1864, a journalist asked him how long it would take him to get to Richmond. "I will agree to be there in about four days," Grant answered. "That is, if General Lee becomes a party to the agreement. But if he objects, the trip will undoubtedly be prolonged."

During May and June 1864, Grant used the telegraph to direct and coordinate the overall war effort. He also engaged Lee in several battles in Virginia as he drove toward Richmond. From May 4-7, Union and Confederate forces clashed at the Wilderness. On the night of May 6, after the Confederates had routed two brigades on the Union right, a Union brigadier general rode up to Grant's headquarters in a panic and blurted that Lee was behind him and the Army of the Potomac was doomed. Grant replied: "Oh, I am heartily tired of hearing what Lee is going to do. Some of you always seem to think he is suddenly going to turn a double somersault, and land in our rear and on both our flanks at the same time. Go back to your command, and try to think what we are going to do ourselves, instead of what Lee is going to do."

Grant suffered a temporary setback in the brutal Wilderness fighting but, unlike previous Union generals in the east, who usually stopped after a defeat, and sometimes after a victory, he pressed on toward Virginia's capital. There was a rapid succession of bloody battles in the spring of 1864. Grant and Lee clashed at Spotsylvania (May 8–19), the North Anna River (May 23–26), and Cold Harbor (June 3). Cold Harbor, in which Grant took seven thousand casualties, became controversial. Grant was accused of being a "butcher" willing

The bloody battle of Cold Harbor renewed criticism of Grant's decision making. *(Library of Congress)*

to sacrifice men in a mindless "war of attrition" (a gradual wearing down of strength and morale). But Grant rejected the charge. Instead, he accepted responsibility for making a mistake. "I have always regretted that the last assault at Cold Harbor was made," he wrote in his *Memoirs.* "At Cold Harbor no advantage whatever was gained to compensate for the heavy loss we sustained."

In the West, Grant had used similar assault tactics. It was only at Vicksburg, with its entrenched fortifications, that he had resorted to feints and other stratagems. In the East, where entrenched defenses were more common, Grant learned he had to adjust his straight attack strategy. After his first attack on Petersburg (June 15–

18)—in which he incurred some eleven thousand casualties in frontal attacks during three days of fighting—Grant abandoned frontal assaults on positions thought to be well defended.

Although Lee often frustrated Grant's attacks tactically, Grant always kept his broader, strategic initiative foremost in his mind. He persisted in trying to pin Lee in place, disrupt his communications, and keep the pressure on his diminishing and exhausted army, while his other armies in the Shenandoah Valley, Middle Tennessee, Georgia, and the Carolinas gnawed away at the Confederacy from the inside.

"My own opinion," Grant informed Sherman, "is that Lee is averse to going out of Virginia and if the cause of the South is lost, he wants Richmond to be the last place surrendered. If he has such views, it may be well to indulge him until we have everything else in our hands."

At the end of June, Grant began a siege on Petersburg, Virginia, that lasted until April 3, 1865. Petersburg was just to the south of Richmond; if it fell, the Confederate capital would soon follow. Lee had finally been run to ground. The dynamic war of movement in the east that had gripped the attention of both sides since the first battle of Bull Run now settled into a long period of immobility. The first years in the east had been similar to the Mexican War—rapid troop movements, battle and retreat, the gradual development of a new battle in places such as Fredericksburg, Chancellorsville, and

This drawing by Edwin Forbes, a famous military sketch artist, lays out and labels the various strategic positions during the siege of Petersburg. *(Library of Congress)*

Gettysburg. Now it had entered a new phase of fighting characterized by trenches, tunnels, and long sieges punctuated by artillery bombardments and quick attempts to overrun earthen fortifications. This last stage of the American Civil War foreshadowed the horrific, static trench warfare of World War I.

From his encampment at nearby Bermuda Hundred Landing, at the confluence of the James and Appomattox Rivers, Grant launched a series of intermittent offensives into lightly defended and unfortified areas north of the James River and south of Petersburg. Notable among them were his Fourth Offensive (August 14–25), in which he succeeded in cutting the Weldon and Petersburg Railroad, a vital link connecting Richmond and the rest of the Confederacy, and his Fifth Offensive (September 29–October 13), a drive on Richmond, which the Confederates thwarted with a valiant stand at Fort Gilmer. In Grant's Sixth Offensive (October 27-28), Grant tried and failed to skirt Lee's defenses near Hatcher's Run, west of Petersburg, and sever the Southside Railroad, the South's last rail link through Petersburg to Richmond. Sometimes winning, sometimes losing, the long-range goal of starving Lee and the Confederacy into submission was slowly coming to pass.

When winter set in, mobile operations in Virginia fell off. The fighting reverted to siege warfare and artillery duels. By the end of 1864, both sides held about the same lines as they had in August, but Lee was much weaker. Grant had an abundance of men, weapons, and supplies. All were short on the Confederate side.

In the meantime, much more activity was occurring elsewhere during the autumn and winter of 1864-1865. On October 19, Sheridan's Army of the Shenandoah—which had been devastating the Shenandoah Valley—defeated Confederate Lieutenant General Jubal A. Early's Army of the Valley at Cedar Creek, Virginia. Sheridan's victory drove the Confederates from the valley, which had provided them most of their food and other supplies. Three weeks later, on November 8, President Lincoln was reelected. The following week, Major General William T. Sherman, who had seized Atlanta earlier in the fall, left the burning city behind and began his now famous March to the Sea. Sherman and his men lived off the land and moved fast, cutting a fifty-mile-wide swath of destruction along his three-hundred-mile journey to Savannah.

In Tennessee, after consistent urging from Grant, Army of the Cumberland commander Major General

This painting, entitled *Grant and his Generals,* by the Norwegian artist Ole Peter Hansen Balling, was painted after Balling spent five weeks with General Grant at City Point, Virginia, sketching officers in the field. Balling did his studies for Philip Sheridan while in the Shenandoah Valley and William T. Sherman and George Henry Thomas while in Washington after the war. The image of George Armstrong Custer, at the far left, is thought to be the only life portrait made of him.

George H. Thomas inflicted a crushing defeat on General John B. Hood's Army of Tennessee on December 16 and forced the Confederates to flee into Mississippi. Five days later, Sherman occupied Savannah. In a wire to the White House, the jubilant Sherman wrote: "To his Excellency President Lincoln: I beg to present you, as a Christmas gift, the city of Savannah, with 150 guns and plenty of ammunition, and also about 35,000 bales of cotton." Sherman's ability to course through Georgia virtually unopposed validated Grant's strategy of coordinated attacks. The South simply could not field enough manpower to oppose Grant and Sheridan in Virginia, Thomas in the West, and Sherman in the deep South. The year 1864 ended on a high note for Grant and the Union.

Eighteen sixty-five began with an attack on Fort Fisher, which guarded the entrance to the harbor at Wilmington, North Carolina. After a two-day naval bombardment, Major General Alfred H. Terry and a Union provisional force of eight thousand men captured the fort on January 15. In the battle of Hatcher's Run (February 5–7), Grant tried—again unsuccessfully—to sever the Southside Railway, but did force Lee to again extend his lines, which thinned out his defenses. While the battle raged, President Jefferson Davis appointed General Robert E. Lee commander of all Confederate armies. Two weeks later, on February 22, Terry's assault force seized Wilmington, the last major port open to the South. One Confederate soldier called the loss of the city "the last rays of departing hope" for the Confederacy. Terry's contingent then joined Major General John Schofield's 23 Corps on an inland march to link up with Sherman's northward-bound army at Goldsboro, North Carolina, on March 23.

By the beginning of March 1865, it had become apparent that the end of the war was near. Most of Sheridan's veteran Shenandoah victors had rejoined Grant, and Grant's other armies threatened Virginia from the northwest, the west, and the south. From his main headquarters and supply base at City Point, on the James River northeast of Petersburg, Grant had fulfilled his duties as general in chief, coordinating the movements of all his armies, while at the same time keeping the pressure on Robert E. Lee's Army of Northern Virginia.

By the end of March, Grant had decided on his last plan of attack to bring the war to an end. As usual, it was to be a coordinated effort, as Grant explained later: "Sheridan reached City Point on the 26th day of March. . . . In preparing his instructions I contemplated just what took place; that is to say, capturing Five Forks [south-west of Petersburg], driving the enemy from Petersburg and Richmond and terminating the contest before separating from the enemy."

Grant began his final onslaught of March 29. On April 1, Sheridan, with twelve thousand cavalrymen reinforced by Major General Gouverneur K. Warren's 5 Corps of sixteen thousand men, attacked Confederate Major General George E. Pickett's entrenched army of some nineteen thousand infantry and cavalry at Five Forks. Sheridan defeated his outnumbered and outgunned adversary decisively and seized the Southside Railroad. Lee was finally forced to evacuate Richmond and Petersburg during the night of April 2–3 and flee south toward North Carolina.

Anticipating Lee's movements, Grant positioned his forces, including cavalry, to the south of Lee's army to block his retreat south. In desperation, Lee turned his army westward. He hoped to cross the Appomattox River, destroy the bridges behind him, and find food for his starving troops in the rich Shenandoah Valley. He then hoped to follow the Richmond and Danville Railroad into North Carolina, where he might join forces with Joe Johnston's beleaguered army, which had been

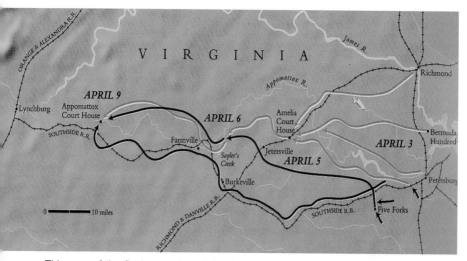

This map of the final campaign of the Civil War, which ended in Appomattox, shows Lee's forces, in red, fleeing from Petersburg and Richmond and Grant's forces, in black, pursuing.

decimated fighting a rearguard action against Sherman. But Grant moved quickly to cut off his retreat. Sheridan arrived at the Richmond and Danville Railroad at Jetersburg on April 5, ruling out Lee's use of the railway.

Lee's last hope was to press on west toward Lynchburg, where the Virginia and Tennessee Railroad met the Southside and the Virginia Central. But on April 6, Grant cut off and captured Lee's rear guard at Sayler's Creek, a tributary of the Appomattox River east of Farmville. In a brutal battle with Sheridan's cavalry corps, the Confederates lost somewhere between seven and eight thousand men, most of whom were captured. The losses represented about a third of what remained of Lee's Army of Northern Virginia.

Grant viewed his adversary's plight and decided that the time had come to address him. At 5:00 PM on

April 7, Grant sent a message to Lee from Farmville: "General: The results of the last week must convince you of the hopelessness of further resistance on the part of the Army of Northern Virginia in this struggle. I feel that it is so, and regard it as my duty to shift from myself the responsibility of any further effusion of blood, by asking of you the surrender of that portion of the Confederate States army known as the Army of Northern Virginia."

Lee replied that same evening: "Though not entertaining the opinion you express of the hopelessness of further resistance on the part of the Army of Northern Virginia, I reciprocate your desire to avoid useless effusion of blood." He went on to ask Grant for his terms. Grant offered to meet with him.

By daybreak of April 9, 1865, Grant's forces had established blocking positions on Lee's southern flank at Appomattox Station. At 5:00 AM, Major General John B. Gordon led a Confederate corps in an attempt to open the way to Lynchburg, but the Federals beat back this last attack of the Army of Northern Virginia. At 8:00 AM, Gordon informed Lee: "I have fought my Corps to a frazzle, and I fear I can do nothing more unless I am heavily supported by Longstreet's Corps." At about the same time, word came from Longstreet that he had just come under heavy attack from Meade's 2 and 6 Corps.

The end had finally come. Lee sent a note to Grant, stating, in part: "I now request an interview in accordance with the offer contained in your letter of yesterday for that purpose." The two great protagonists in the defining conflict of the United States of America met at two o'clock that afternoon at the house of Wilmer McLean, a resident of Appomattox Court House.

Grant, who had to travel the greatest distance, was the last to arrive. Displaying his customary indifference to clothes—much like his early mentor, Zachary Taylor—he was dressed in an unbuttoned, mud-splashed, dark blue tunic. He wore riding boots but no belt, sword, or spurs. His adversary's appearance posed a study in contrasts, as Grant himself later described Lee: "General Lee was dressed in a full uniform which was entirely new, and was wearing a sword of considerable value . . . In my rough traveling suit, the uniform of a private with the straps of a lieutenant-general, I must have contrasted very strangely with a man so handsomely dressed, six feet high and of faultless form. But this was not a matter that I thought of until afterwards."

The two warriors then slipped into a pleasant conversation reminiscing about their mutual service in Mexico, until Lee reminded Grant of the purpose of their meeting and requested his terms for surrender. Grant obliged with generous terms, much like those Taylor had proposed years before at Monterrey. He paroled all Confederate officers and men if they agree to not to take up arms again. In addition, as Grant wrote out in triplicate, he required: "The arms, artillery and public property to be parked and stacked, and turned over to the officers appointed by me to receive them. This will not embrace

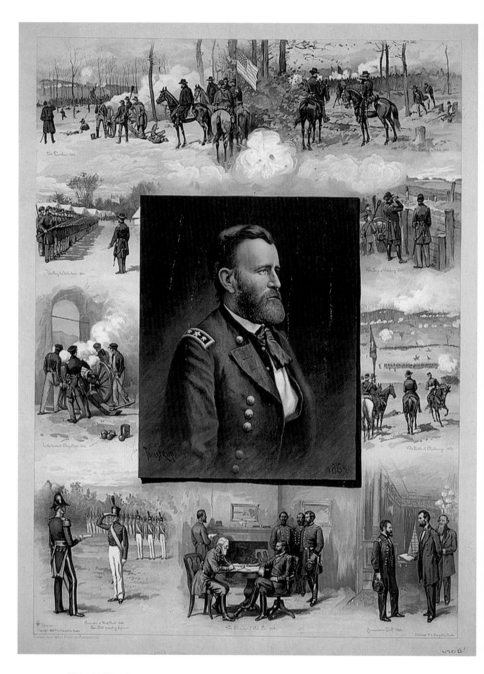

This 1885 print shows Grant surrounded by nine scenes of his career from his West Point graduation in 1843 to Lee's surrender in 1865, including an artillery crew in the Tower of Chapultepec, Mexico, 1847; drilling volunteers, 1861; Fort Donelson, 1862; Shiloh, 1862; the Siege of Vicksburg, 1863; Chattanooga, 1863; and his appointment by Lincoln as Union Commander, 1864. *(Library of Congress)*

the side-arms of the officers, nor their private horses or baggage. This done, each officer and man will be allowed to return to his home, not to be disturbed by the United States authority so long as they observe their paroles and the laws in force where they may reside."

When Lee read the part allowing his officers to keep their swords, he said, "This will have a very happy effect on my army," and agreed to Grant's terms.

After the historic meeting at Appomattox, Lee's aide, Colonel Charles Marshall, commented, "There was no theatrical display about it. It was in itself perhaps the greatest tragedy that ever occurred in the history of the world, but it was the simplest, plainest, and most thoroughly devoid of any attempt at effect, that you can imagine."

One of those present at the signing was Lieutenant General James Longstreet, one of Lee's chief commanders and Grant's old friend. Years later, Longstreet recalled, "[T]he first thing that General Grant said to me when we stepped aside, placing his arm in mine, was: 'Pete, let's have another game of brag [an old-time game], to recall the old days which were so pleasant to us all.' His whole greeting and conduct was as though nothing had ever happened to mar our pleasant relations."

Chief Executive

Grant returned to Washington on Thursday morning, April 13, 1865. After the capture of Lee's army at Appomattox, he felt sure that "all the armies of the rebels will in due time surrender," which they did. The bloodiest war in American history—one that would ultimately claim more than a million casualties—was for all practical purposes over. It was time, Grant figured, to stop wasting money on a war that was won, to reduce the size of the army, and to start the healing process of a wounded nation.

The next day, Grant met with President Lincoln and his cabinet to discuss the future of the South. After the meeting, Lincoln invited the general and Mrs. Grant to attend a performance of *Our American Cousin* at Ford's Theater that night with him and Mrs. Lincoln. Grant,

Just before his death, Lincoln met with some of his top advisors to discuss reconstruction of the South. Here he is pictured with Sherman, Grant, and Admiral Porter.

having already made plans to visit two of his children at their school in Burlington, New Jersey, respectfully declined. That evening, at a stopover in Philadelphia, Grant received a telegram. It read, in part: "The President was assassinated at Ford's Theatre at 10 30 tonight & cannot live . . . " After escorting Julia and his son Jesse to Burlington and assuring their safety, Grant hurried back to Washington.

By the time Grant arrived in the capital, Lincoln was dead and Andrew Johnson, a self-educated southerner of modest beginnings, had been sworn in as president. At Lincoln's funeral service, Grant wept openly for the loss of "incontestably the greatest man I ever knew."

Even as he mourned, Grant was apprehensive about Lincoln's successor and how Johnson would deal with the reconstruction of the South. He did not know why, Grant told Julia, but "for some reason I dread the change."

In late 1865, President Johnson asked Grant to tour the South and to report on his findings. Grant was surprised at the cordial reception he received in the conquered South. His report to Johnson recommended a lenient Reconstruction policy, but that every possible effort needed to be taken to keep the former slaves from being forced back into slavery. At first, the president seemed to share Grant's opinions, but Grant soon came to feel that Johnson's policies permitted Southern states to infringe on the rights of blacks.

At issue was the question of how the Southern states were going to begin the process of being readmitted to the Union and how they were going to adjust to the radical economic and social changes that followed the Thirteenth Amendment, which once and for all ended legal slavery. Those members of the Republican party known as Radical Republicans worried that, without careful planning, power in the South would revert to the same wealthy landowners who had held it before the war began. Johnson made some attempts to impose strict penalties on that population, but efforts to extend po-litical power to former slaves were hampered at every step. White southerners used the so-called black codes to maintain control of former slaves. These were statues passed by individual states which effectively negated the advances promised by the federal government. Principally, the codes were directed toward keeping African Americans from voting or owning land. Johnson incensed the Radical Republicans and others in the North by ignoring these codes and by offering large-scale,

President Andrew Johnson.

blanket pardons to former Confederates who had been elected to return to Congress.

When Congress convened in December of 1865, the leadership refused to allow the representatives elected from the South to take their seats. Congress was dominated by Radical Republicans who thought the Southern elections had been conducted unfairly and that Johnson was not doing enough to restore order to the South. A legislative battle ensued. Congress emerged victorious; Johnson's power was weakening.

In June 1866, Congress proposed the Fourteenth Amendment, which was ratified in 1868. Among other things, the amendment granted citizenship to former slaves and required states to extend due process of law

and equal protection of the laws to all persons. President
Johnson encouraged the former Confederate states to
reject it, and they did, but to no avail. Though Grant had
attempted to steer clear of politics before, he was one
of many people opposed to Johnson's policies.

INDIAN AFFAIRS

During the Vicksburg campaign, Grant had shocked many
members of the officer corps by appointing Ely Parker, a full-
blooded Seneca Indian, to his wartime staff. At the time, most white
people distrusted Native Americans and considered them backward
and immoral. An innate sense of national guilt over dispossessing
them of their native land worsened the deep and widespread
prejudice against them.

Parker, a qualified civil engineer before he ever met Grant, served
as the general's aide and secretary. Parker's education opened the door
to his success in the Union Army, but it was only possible because
Grant rejected the prevailing prejudice of his time. He eventually
promoted Parker to brevet brigadier general. Shortly after Grant
became president, he appointed Parker commissioner of Indian
affairs and established a Board of Indian Commissioners, with the
intent of totally renovating existing government policies toward
Native Americans.

Although the Fourteenth Amendment granted citizenship to
anyone born within the borders of the United States, its provisions
excluded native peoples living on reservations. Their relationship with
the government was based on some 370 treaties. White men broke
most of them, the Native Americans the rest. At the same time,
crooked agents profited from rake-offs of government supplies
meant for the Native Americans and looked on indifferently while
families went hungry.

Grant persuaded Congress to increase the appropriation for

Indian affairs from $5 million to $7 million, channeling the extra money into education and training. Moreover, to curb the corruption among the agents, he dismissed almost all of them when he took office. Acting on the advice of the Board of Indian Commissioners, Grant abolished the treaty system of dealing with the tribes. Instead, he mandated that all Native Americans would from then on be considered wards of the government, which, in other words, made the government responsible for their well being. The consequences of that decision reverberate today.

On July 25, 1866, in recognition of Grant's past and continuing contributions to his nation, the Senate confirmed him as general of the army, the first American officer to attain four-star ranking. His new rank afforded him financial stability, and he could often be seen tooling about the streets of Washington in a light buggy drawn by a spirited horse. An army of well-wishers lavished him with gifts. The cities of Philadelphia and Galena each bought him a house, and a fund drive on his behalf yielded enough money to buy an expensive house at 205 I Street in Georgetown, with cash and a healthy investment in bonds to spare.

In August, the president took his case against the Fourteenth Amendment to the people during a two-week tour of the Midwest. To capitalize on Grant's popularity, Johnson insisted that Grant join him. Everywhere they went, crowds chanted, "Grant, Grant, Grant." When one of Johnson's aides told a crowd that Grant supported Johnson, Grant sternly rebuked him. "No man is authorized to speak for me in political matters," he said, "and

I ask you to desist." To his wife, Julia, he confided, "I have never been so tired of anything before as I have been with the political stump speeches of Mr. Johnson. I look upon them as a national disgrace." The tour did little to enhance Johnson's position but did much to elevate Grant's image in the political arena. Both Democrats and Republicans saw him as a very electable presidential candidate.

Despite growing misgivings about Johnson and his policies, Grant respected the office of commander in chief. He did his best to work with him harmoniously. But in the summer of 1867, Johnson became embroiled in another dispute with Congress over the power of the president to remove members of his own cabinet, and Grant could not avoid taking a side. He wrote an angry letter to Johnson, rebuking him for his attempts to outmaneuver Congress. When that letter became public, Republicans across the nation sided with the general.

On February 24, 1868, matters came to a head when the House of Representatives voted to impeach President Johnson. Grant favored their action—chiefly, as he confessed to one senator, because Johnson was "such an infernal liar." The attempt failed when the Senate, acting as a court of impeachment, acquitted Johnson by a single vote on May 16. Although he survived impeachment, Johnson was dead politically. The 1868 presidential race was wide-open.

Less than a week after Johnson was acquitted by the Senate, Republicans nominated Ulysses S. Grant for

THE GREAT AMERICAN TANNER.

This political cartoon from the 1868 election invokes Grant's humble beginnings as a tanner in Galena, as well as his successful military career. On the left, popular New York governer John Thompson Hoffman presents Grant with two Democratic candidates for president. On the right, three Confederate generals acknowledge their defeat by Grant. *(Library of Congress)*

president at their convention in Chicago, with Speaker of the House Schuyler Colfax as his running mate. Grant accepted the nomination in a letter that called for an end to partisan politics and bickering. "Let us have peace," he implored. The words became his campaign slogan, and they carried him to victory in the fall over his Democratic opponent, Governor Horatio Seymour of New York.

Grant heard the election results at Congressman Elihu B. Washburne's house, after which he walked home in the early morning hours of November 4, 1868, where he found Julia, eager to hear the results, waiting for him at the front door. "I am afraid I am elected," he told her. In that day's edition of the *New York Sun*, editor and part owner Charles A. Dana wrote an editorial summarizing Grant's achievement and what it meant to the nation: "The election of Gen. GRANT is the finale of an eight years' struggle, which has teamed with events without parallel in the annals of this or any other nation. . . . Starting in obscurity, and advancing by slow and sure steps, he has reached an eminence where he challenges the respect and the confidence of his countrymen and has made his name a household word throughout the nation. . . . [N]o candid person will for a moment doubt that the interests, the honor, and the glory of the Republic are secure in his hands."

The obscure country boy from Point Pleasant, Ohio—upon whose small shoulders Abraham Lincoln had thrust the weight and fate of the Republic—had himself risen to the peak of national power and personal attainment. On March 4, 1869, Ulysses S. Grant took the oath of office to become the eighteenth president and commander in chief of the United States of America.

In his inaugural address, he set the tone for his presidency. "The responsibilities of the position I feel; but accept them without fear," he said. "The office has come to me unsought; I commence its duties untrammeled. I bring to it a conscious desire and determination to fill it to the best of my ability to the satisfaction of the people." At age forty-six, he became the youngest man elected president to that point.

On November 7, 1869, Grant moved into the White House with his beloved Julia, their daughter, Nellie, and, individually and intermittently, their three sons. The Grants lived reclusively at times and entertained lavishly on other occasions. A typical day would see him arise early and read the newspapers until breakfast. After a morning walk, he would conduct official business from his office until 3:00 PM, then take a carriage ride or another stroll until dinner. After dining, Grant spent his evenings reading more newspapers or visiting with friends until 10:00 or 11:00 PM—except when hosting sumptuous dinners replete with dozens of courses and fine French wines.

Grant's presidency would be dominated by a few key political issues. First was the limited power of the office. Johnson's administration had soured Congress and weakened the office to one of its lowest points ever. Although Grant was widely admired and respected, even credited with saving the Union, this weak-

Grant during his presidency. *(National Portrait Gallery, Washington, D.C.)*

ened position made it difficult to sway much influence over Congress or the bureaucracy.

It was a time of great change. Six of the eleven former Confederate states were readmitted to the Union in the summer of 1868—the remaining four would return two years later. But the fallout from the Civil War would be felt for years to come. There was a huge debt left from the war. Grant made efforts to stabilize the country's finances. Because of the vast amounts of money that had been spent during the war, the size of government had grown rapidly. This inevitably led to corruption as dishonest manufacturers and others found ways to sell shoddy goods or to attempt financial manipulations. Grant made some attempts to clean up the corruption but it had taken root and would plague him and his administration.

Grant soon discovered that running a government was a very different job than fielding an army. The chain of command he was used to, when it was possible to issue an order and have it be carried out, simply did not exist in the maze of bureaucracy. Matters were made worse by Grant's inexperience as a politician. His choice of cabinet and other key positions reflected his political naiveté. Instead of selecting strong leaders of his party, he appointed personal friends and wealthy campaign contributors. Critics ridiculed most of Grant's cabinet choices as a mixture of excellence, mediocrity, and inexplicable happenstance.

Grant did make one particularly inspired political

appointment when he placed Hamilton Fish, a cultured elder statesman, as Secretary of State. Fish would negotiate American's foreign policy with skill and aplomb. He kept the young country, exhausted and broke after the bitter conflict, out of a potential war with Spain and ef-

Grant's choice for secretary of state, Hamilton Fish. *(Library of Congress)*

fected a long-lasting peace with Great Britain.

The national debt had ballooned from $64 million in 1861 to $2.8 billion in 1869. The new chief executive believed the debt should be paid in full in order to protect the country's credit rating, and that there should be a return to hard currency—money secured by either gold or silver deposits. "The payment of this *principal* and *interest*, as well as the return to a specie basis [gold or silver], as soon as it can be accomplished without material detriment to the debtor class, must be provided for," he said at his inaugural. Two weeks later, on March 18, 1869, he signed the Act to Strengthen the Public Credit, the first law of his administration. The law pledged to pay all bondholders in "gold or its equivalent," and to redeem paper money—greenback currency issued during the war— "at the earliest practicable period." In another early move intended to curb the rampant political corruption at all levels of government, Grant appointed the first Civil Service Commission but abandoned it in the face of Congressional obstructionism. Once again, Congress's uneasy relationship with the office of the presidency hampered efforts at reform.

Next to the economy, Grant's greatest domestic problems centered in the South. He and his administration worked to settle differences between the North and the South. In his approach to Reconstruction, Grant generally adhered to Radical-Republican goals of providing African Americans the full rights of citizenship, particularly the right to vote, and defeating the black codes that had been passed during Johnson's administration. In 1869, Congress proposed the Fifteenth Amendment, which was ratified the following year. It declared that the rights of U.S. citizens to vote "shall not be denied or abridged by the United States or by any State on account of race, color, or previous condition of servitude." The intent was to make all forms of racial injustice illegal and to keep local and state governments from mandating a form of second-class citizenship to the former slaves. But Southern states would continue to get around the amendment for many years thereafter by initiating white primaries, poll taxes, literacy or property tests, or residence and registration requirements. Worse yet, the amendment led to an increase in terrorist

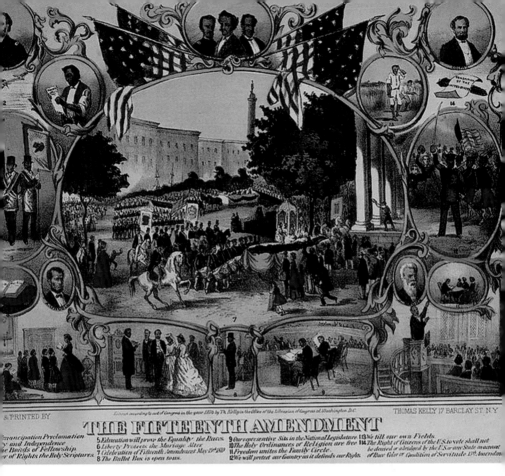

THE FIFTEENTH AMENDMENT

:mancipation Proclamation   5 Education will prove the Equality of the Races.   9 Our representative Sits in the National Legislature. 13 We till our own Fields.
y and Independence   6 Liberty Protects the Marriage Alter.   10 The Holy Ordinances or Religion are free. 14 The Right of Citizens of the U.S to vote shall not
e Bonds of Fellowship.   7 Celebration of Fifteenth Amendment May 19 1870   11 Freedom unites the Family Circle.   be denied or abridged by the U.S or any State on account
r of Rights the Holy Scriptures. 8 The Ballot Box is open to us.   12 We will protect our Country as it defends our Rights. of Race Color or Condition of Servitude 15th, Amendmt

This celebratory print, made in honor of the enactment of the Fifteenth Amendment on March 30, 1870, shows the grand parade in Baltimore celebrating the amendment's ratification, surrounded by portraits of the amendment's supporters and vignettes illustrating the rights granted by its passage. *(Library of Congress)*

acts against blacks by the Ku Klux Klan (KKK), a group devoted to restoring white domination over newly freed blacks.

To curb the violence perpetrated by Klansmen, Grant urged Congress to intervene: "I urgently recommend such legislation, as in the judgment of Congress, shall effectually secure life, liberty, and property, and the enforcement of law, in all parts of the United States." Congress obliged and enacted the Ku Klux Klan bill, one of three so-called force bills, on April 20, 1871. These three laws threatened stiff penalties for anyone caught violating the letter or the spirit of the Fifteenth Amendment. They gave the president broad powers of enforcement, including the right to use federal troops if necessary. Southerners were already upset about the presence of federal troops in the South and these force bills only heightened tensions in the region.

In a proclamation, Grant implored the people of the South to comply with the law voluntarily and to help suppress the Klan and its activities. Otherwise, he noted, if the violence continued, he would act promptly and decisively to protect "citizens of every race and color" in the "peaceful enjoyment of the rights guaranteed to them by the Constitution." After a series of violent incidents in early May, Grant backed his words and sent federal troops to the South to help federal officials "arrest and break up bands of disguised night marauders." Grant's willingness to act paid off with the return of some three-thousand grand-jury indictments in 1871. Klan activities fell off dramatically by 1872, which prompted the *National Republican* to report, "There has never been a leader in the White House who has been more uniformly fair to all races and classes of men."

Though his administration had made some achievements, Grant was not able to become a strong president. The country was changing rapidly—railroads were booming, industry was growing again, and what became known as the Gilded Age, a time of great accumulation of wealth, had begun. After the sacrifice demanded by first the struggle over the expansion of slavery and then the war, many wanted to focus on making money and making up for the lost years. Northerners grew weary of dealing with white racism in the South. Many had fought the war to preserve the Union; freeing the slaves had not been their first priority.

As the 1872 election approached, a group of Republicans opposed to Grant's plan for Reconstruction, and concerned about political corruption, formed a splinter group they called the Liberal Republicans. In a convention in May of 1872 in Cincinnati, they nominated Horace Greeley, the eccentric editor of the *New York Tribune,* as their candidate for president. When the Democrats convened later that year, they also nominated Greeley.

Six weeks later, on June 5, 1872, the official Republican Party met in Philadelphia and renominated Grant on the first ballot. Over the course of the presidential campaign, the Liberal Republicans and the Democrats could not work in harmony toward a common goal, whereas the campaign machinery of Grant's Republicans ran smoothly. On November 5, Grant—running with vice-presidential candidate Henry Wilson, the junior senator from Massachusetts—won reelection by a wider margin than he had won by in his first election.

In his second inaugural address on March 4, 1873, Grant said, in part: "I acknowledge before this assemblage . . . the obligation I am under to my countrymen for the great honor they have conferred on me by returning me to the highest office within their gift, and the further obligation resting on me to render to them the best services within my power. This I promise, looking forward with the greatest anxiety to the day when I shall be released from responsibilities that at times are almost overwhelming, and from which I have scarcely had a respite since the eventful firing upon Fort Sumter, in April 1861, to the present day . . . I have been the subject of abuse and slander scarcely ever equaled in political history, which to-day I feel that I can afford to disregard in view of your verdict, which I gratefully accept as my vindication."

He might have seen his reelection as a vindication, but Grant's second term began in a storm of controversy. During the presidential campaign, the *New York Sun* revealed what came to be known as the Crédit Mobilier scandal—an attempt by directors of the Union Pacific Railroad to pirate company funds and buy favors in Congress with part of their ill-gotten gains. To work their scheme, the directors acquired Crédit Mobilier, a dummy firm in Pennsylvania, to use as a corporate shield. They then proceeded to funnel off Union Pacific money for phony construction services never rendered. The *Sun's* story set a congressional investigation in motion, which resulted in the censure or expulsion of several members of Congress in early 1873. Neither Grant, his associates, nor his allies in Congress were implicated in the scandal—the illegal dealings had actually taken place before Grant's first term in office—but critics attempted to lay blame on Grant.

In the autumn of the same year, the great economic boom that followed the Civil War ended with a deadening thud. The Panic of 1873 began with the failure of three Wall Street financial institutions in mid-September, principally the firm of Jay Cooke & Company, which was then heralded as the rock of American financial institutions. The company had kept the Union solvent during the war and was underwriting construction of the Northern Pacific Railroad at the time of its collapse. Financial pandemonium followed, forcing the New York Stock Exchange to shut down for ten trading days. Bankruptcies became commonplace, industries closed their doors, farmers lost their land, commerce came to a standstill, unemployment skyrocketed, and the nation plunged into a severe depression.

Washington politicians immediately pressured Grant to inflate the nation's paper currency by issuing more unredeemable greenbacks—paper money not backed by gold or silver, which the government had issued to finance the Civil War. When Grant refused to inflate the currency, Congress approved an inflation bill to add $18 million to the paper currency already in circulation. In April 1874, Grant vetoed the bill, calling the measure "a departure from the principles of finance, national interest, the nation's obligations to creditors, Congressional promises, party pledges (on the part of both political parties), and of personal views and promises made by me in every annual message sent to Congress and in each inaugural address." His strong stance against inflating the currency led Congress to pass the Specie Resumption Act, which made greenbacks redeemable in gold or silver. ("Specie" means "money in coin.") Grant signed the bill on January 14, 1875, and the nation returned to solvency.

Grant's political problems were sometimes because of his own mistakes, but more often were due to his misplaced trust in friends and high-ranking appointees. For years, a group of corrupt officials and businessmen, known collectively as the "Whiskey Ring," had been bilking the government out of revenue money derived from taxes placed on whiskey by the Lincoln Administration to help pay for the Civil War. After a long, ongoing investigation, the money trail led back to Orville E. Babcock, Grant's principal secretary. Grant received

Orville E. Babcock was not only an important member of Grant's administration, but also one of his right-hand-men during the war.

evidence of Babcock's involvement in the ring with disbelief, but he ordered, "Let no guilty man escape." Further investigation revealed that evidence against Babcock was circumstantial, and a jury acquitted him, largely because of Grant's favorable testimony. Nevertheless, the investigation ultimately compromised several of Grant's appointees, which made Grant's character suspect by association. Echoing similar charges levied during the war, rumors spread that Grant was drinking and not fully in control of his administration.

Hamilton Fish, himself a man of unimpeachable honesty, defended Grant to the cabinet as "the most scrupulously truthful man I ever met." He told *New York Herald* reporter John Russell Young, "I do not think it would have been possible for Grant to have told a lie, even if he had composed it and written it down." Despite Grant's reputation for honesty and integrity, the Whiskey Ring scandal left an indelible stain on Grant's presidency. On May 29, 1875, Grant issued a letter to the public stating he would not be a candidate for a third term. He was still president, however, and his problems continued.

On March 2, 1876, the House of Representatives impeached Secretary of War William W. Belknap on charges that he had accepted bribes. Belknap tendered his resignation to Grant, and Grant accepted it. Since Belknap was no longer a government official, the Senate ruled that it had no power to convict him. Belknap went free, and Grant was reviled as having orchestrated Belknap's escape from punishment.

At year's end, Grant delivered his last address to Congress on December 2, 1876, in which he reviewed his performance in the White House:

> It was my fortune, or misfortune, to be called to the office of Chief Executive without any previous political

training. . . . Under such circumstances it is but reasonable to suppose that errors of judgment must have occurred [in appointing government administrators]. . . . History shows that no Administration from the time of [George] Washington to the present has been free from these mistakes. But I leave comparisons to history, claiming only that I have acted in every instance from a conscientious desire to do what was right, constitutional, within the law, and for the very best interests of the whole people. Failures have been errors of judgment, not of intent.

Grant retired as the nation's chief executive on March 4, 1877. In the end, despite his good intentions, his terms in office had diminished his reputation. The overall impression was one of inability to deal with the massive social issues left after the Civil War and of unseemly corruption. Though Grant made some efforts to protect the rights of African Americans, abuses—particularly in the South—continued. He made attempts to deal with the problems facing Native Americans, but establishing the Bureau of Indian Affairs did not stop the slaughter and dispossession happening in the west. His sometimes difficult relationship with Congress only exacerbated the weaknesses of Grant's administration. The directness and aggression that made Grant an effective general were neutralized by political bureaucracy. The final impression of U. S. Grant the president is one of a man in over his head.

Republican Rutherford B. Hayes succeeded Grant in the White House. Grant told his friend John Russell Young, "I was never as happy in my life as the day I left the White House. I felt like a boy getting out of school." Free from government service at last, he spent the next two years sailing around the world with Julia. When Grant returned from his long voyage, the Republicans tried to nominate him for a third term when Hayes declined to run again, but a split in the party resulted in the nomination of James A. Garfield. Grant's political career was over.

Grant remained a public figure, however, and his friends sponsored a subscription drive to raise money in appreciation of his long public service. He used the money to buy a house in New York City at 3 East 66th Street and invested the rest with his son's Wall Street firm. Unfortunately for both of them, Ulysses Jr.'s partner was dishonest. The firm crashed in 1884 and the Grants lost all their money. A story about the firm's failure in the *New York Tribune* concluded: "It is not believed that the ex-president knew the state of the firm's affairs." Once again, Grant's good intentions had been betrayed.

Faced with an urgent need to find some means of support, Grant agreed to write his memoirs for Samuel L. Clemens (Mark Twain), who was then a subscription book publisher. He began the work with a quote from *Imitation of Christ*, by the fifteenth-century mystic Thomas à Kempis: "Man proposes and God disposes." Perhaps he felt a divine hand on his shoulder, guiding him from obscure beginnings to the acme of personal and public attainment, as he wrote in clear, straight-forward prose, and with amazingly detailed recall of the events of his life.

As he worked on his memoirs a pain developed in his throat. In October 1884, his doctor diagnosed its cause as terminal cancer, the result of years of cigar smoking. Grant raced to finish his manuscript in hopes it would sell well enough to provide for Julia's old age before he died.

In the spring of 1885, Julia took him to a cottage on

This photograph of Grant writing his memoirs in pencil was taken at Drexel Cottage on Mount McGregor only ten days before he died.

Mount McGregor, eleven miles from Saratoga Springs in the Adirondack Mountains. High up in the clear air, wrapped in coats and scarves, Grant spent his days writing. Though he was in a race against time, his memoirs did not suffer. He completed the work, *Personal Memoirs of U.S. Grant*, about a week before he died on July 23, 1885. When it was published, the book became a huge financial—and literary—success, providing Julia with about $450,000 with which to live out her life in comfort. Many literary experts regard Grant's *Memoirs* as the finest military autobiography ever written.

Ulysses Simpson Grant, fighting general and president of the people, was buried in a temporary vault in New York City's Riverside Park. In 1897, on the 75th anniversary of his birth, his remains were moved to Grant's Tomb, a magnificent neoclassical granite mausoleum at Riverside Drive on Morningside Heights in Manhattan. In 1902, Grant's beloved wife, Julia, died and joined him there. The United States Government designated Grant's Tomb a national memorial in 1957—a fitting tribute to the memory of a man who served his country for many years with honor, courage, and dedication.

Timeline

1822   Born on April 27 in Point Pleasant, Ohio.

1839   Enters the United States Military Academy at West Point, New York.

1843   Graduates from West Point; assigned to Jefferson Barracks, Missouri, where he meets Julia Dent.

1846–   Mexican War; serves under Generals Zachary Taylor
1848   and Winfield Scott and participates in most major battles; marries Julia Dent.

1848–   Serves at various army posts in peacetime assignments;
1854   resigns from army with permanent rank of captain.

1861–   Civil War; returns to army as a colonel of volunteers
1865   and progresses to permanent rank of lieutenant general and appointed general in chief of the Union armies; major battles include Forts Henry and Donelson, Shiloh, Vicksburg, Petersburg, and Appomattox.

1866   Commissioned general of the army.

1869   Inaugurated as eighteenth president of the United States.

1873   Inaugurated for second term as president.

1877   Retires from White House.

1877   Travels around the world, through 1879.

1884   Begins *Personal Memoirs of U.S. Grant*, finishes 1885.

1885   Dies at Mount McGregor, New York, on July 23.

1897   Remains interred in Grant's Tomb, overlooking the Hudson River in New York.

Sources

CHAPTER ONE: The Formative Years

p. 12, "He was always . . ." *Interview with Hannah Simpson Grant,* (http://www.mscomm.com/~ulysses/page11.html), 11.

p. 13, "incapable of teaching . . ." *Ulysses S. Grant Chronology,* (http://www.lib.siu.edu/projects/usgrant/grant2.htm), 1.

p. 13, "I can see [him] now . . ." Ibid.

p. 13, "I was not studious . . ." Jean Edward Smith, *Grant* (New York: Simon & Schuster, 2001), 22–23.

p. 14, "[Ulysses] made fearful work . . ." Harry J. Maihafer, *The General and the Journalists: Ulysses S. Grant, Horace Greeley, and Charles Dana* (Washington, DC: Brassey's, 2001), 8.

p. 14, "Horses seem to . . ." *Ulysses S. Grant and His Horses,* (http://www.saints.css.edu/mkelsey/hors1.html), 1.

p. 14, "hold out for over . . ." Maihafer, *The General and the Journalists,* 6.

p. 14, "understands the team . . ." Ibid.

p. 15, "Papa says I may . . ." Grant, *Personal Memoirs,* vol. 1, 30.

p. 15, "From that age . . ." *Ulysses S. Grant Chronology,* 2.

p. 15, "For this I was . . ." Smith, *Grant,* 23.

p. 16, "He was unusually . . ." Maihafer, *The General and the Journalists,* 7.

p. 16, "I believe you . . ." *Ulysses S. Grant Chronology,* 2.

p. 16, "What appointment?" Ibid.

p. 16, "To West Point . . ." Ibid.

p. 16, "A military life . . ." Ulysses S. Grant, *Personal Memoirs of U. S. Grant,* Vol. 1 (Scituate, MA: Digital Scanning, 1998), 38.

p. 16, "for generations, in all . . ." Ibid., 17.

p. 18, "No, it stands for . . ." Maihafer, *The General and the Journalists,* 32.

p. 19, "delicate frame . . ." Smith, *Grant,* 26.

p. 19-20, "a girlish modesty . . ." Ibid.

p. 20, "a noble, generous heart . . ." Ibid.

p. 20, "His hair was . . ." Ibid.

p. 20, "had not the faintest . . ." Grant, *Personal Memoirs,* vol. 1, 38.

p. 21, "I did not take hold . . ." Ibid.

p. 21, "colossal size . . ." Maihafer, *The General and the Journalists,* 33.

p. 22, "the finest specimen . . ." Ibid.

p. 22-23, "My experience in . . ." Grant, *Personal Memoirs,* vol. 1, 41.

p. 23, "The horse increased . . ." Smith, *Grant,* 28.

p. 24, "I was impatient to see . . ." Ibid., 29.

p. 24-25, "Soldier! Will you . . ." Geoffrey Perret, *Ulysses S. Grant: Soldier & President* (New York: Modern Library, 1999), 36.

p. 25, "gave me a distaste . . ." Ibid., 37.

CHAPTER TWO: Love and War Games

p. 26, "a perfect soldier . . ." Trevor N. Dupuy, Curt John, and David L. Bongard, *The Harper Encyclopedia of Military Biography* (New York: HarperCollins, 1992), 396.

p. 26-27, "It did seem to me . . ." Smith, *Grant,* 29.

p. 28, "masterful in his ways . . ." Perret, *Ulysses S. Grant,* 38.

p. 29, "That young man . . ." Smith, *Grant*, 31.

p. 29-30, "After that I do . . ." Grant, *Personal Memoirs*, vol. 1, 46.

p. 31, "For myself, I was. . ." Ibid., 53, 55.

p. 32, "I now discovered . . ." Ibid., 48.

p. 32, "I, child that . . ." Smith, *Grant*, 31.

p. 32, "The great elevation . . ." Ibid., 36.

p. 34, "it was nonsense . . ." Ibid., 38.

p. 34, "on or near the Rio . . ." Ibid.

p. 36, "A better army . . ." Grant, *Personal Memoirs*, vol. 1, 168.

p. 36, "He dressed entirely . . ." Smith, *Grant*, 39.

p. 37, "We were sent . . ." Grant, *Personal Memoirs*, vol. 1, 68.

CHAPTER THREE: The Mexican War

p. 38, "hostilities may now . . ." Smith, *Grant*, 45.

p. 38, "a state of war exists . . ." Ibid.

p. 39-40, "I thought what a fearful . . ." Grant, *Personal Memoirs*, vol. 1, 94.

p. 40, "A ball struck close . . ." Smith, *Grant*, 48.

p. 41, "Cannister and grape . . ." Ibid.

p. 43, "This left no doubt . . ." Grant, *Personal Memoirs*, vol. 1, 98.

p. 43, "I do not know . . ." Perret, *Ulysses S. Grant*, 56-57.

p. 46, "lacking the moral . . ." Maihafer, *The General and the Journalists*, 37.

p. 48, "giving him water . . ." Ibid.

p. 48, "I hope it may . . ." Smith, *Grant*, 58.

p. 48, "He could see . . ." Perret, *Ulysses S. Grant*, 60.

p. 50-51, "For every one . . ." Robert Leckie, *The Wars of America*, Vol. I. Updated Edition (New York: HarperCollins, 1993), 358.

p. 52, "Cerro Gordo is . . ." Grant, *Personal Memoirs*, vol. 1, 131.

p. 53, "The surprise of . . ." Ibid., 133.

p. 54, "The attack was made . . ." Ibid., 132.

p. 58, "He sees everything . . ." Lida Mayo, "The Mexican War and After," in *American Military History,* Vol. 1: 1775–1902 (Edited by Maurice Matloff. Conshohocken, PA: Combined Books, 1996), 178.

p. 58, "Credit is due to . . ." Ibid.

p. 59, "for gallant and . . ." Smith, *Grant,* 71.

p. 60, "Since my last . . ." Ibid., 69.

CHAPTER FOUR: Depression to Secession

p. 62, "I was married . . ." Grant, *Personal Memoirs,* vol. 1, 193.

p. 62, "They considered . . ." Perret, *Ulysses S. Grant,* 82.

p. 63, "where two years . . ." Grant, *Personal Memoirs,* vol. 1, 193.

p. 64, "You know how . . ." Smith, *Grant,* 76.

p. 65, "one-seventh of those . . ." Grant, *Personal Memoirs,* vol. 1, 198.

p. 65, "My dearest, you could . . ." Perret, *Ulysses S. Grant,* 95.

p. 66, "in the states . . ." Smith, *Grant,* 80.

p. 67, "We continued that . . ." Maihafer, *The General and the Journalists,* 54.

p. 68, "A cook could . . ." Ibid.

p. 68, "How forsaken . . ." Perret, *Ulysses S. Grant,* 102.

p. 69, "I saw no chance . . ." Grant, *Personal Memoirs,* vol. 1, 210.

p. 69, "a new struggle . . ." Ibid.

p. 70, "Some of the . . ." Maihafer, *The General and the Journalists,* 59.

p. 70, "the kindest husband . . ." Ibid.

p. 71, "With a Democrat . . ." Grant, *Personal Memoirs,* vol. 1, 215.

p. 74, "the passions of . . ." Ibid.

CHAPTER FIVE: Grant Takes Command

p. 77, "combinations too . . ." Smith, *Grant,* 99.

p. 77-78, "I think I can . . ." Ibid., 100.

p. 79, "I declined to receive . . ." Grant, *Personal Memoirs,* vol. 1, 239.

p. 79, "Anyone who looked . . ." Smith, *Grant,* 105.

p. 80, "In accepting this . . ." Al Kaltman, *Cigars, Whiskey & Winning Leadership Lessons from General Ulysses S. Grant* (Paramus, NJ: Prentice Hall Press, 1998), 36.

p. 81, "This was a view . . ." Arthur L. Conger, *The Rise of U. S. Grant* (New York: Da Capo Press, 1996), 7.

p. 81, "Well, sir, I had no . . ." Bruce Catton, *Grant Moves South* (Edison, NJ: Castle Books, 2000), 17.

p. 85, "The strong arm . . ." Perret, *Ulysses S. Grant,* 139.

p. 86, "The alarm 'surrounded' . . ." Kaltman, *Cigars, Whiskey & Winning,* 54.

p. 87, "With permission . . ." Perret, *Ulysses S. Grant,* 159.

p. 87, "taken and held . . ." Catton, *Grant Moves South,* 131.

p. 89-90, "I shall take and . . ." James Marshal-Cornwall, *Grant As Military Commander* (New York: Barnes & Noble, 1995), 56.

p. 90, "Floyd . . . who was . . ." Grant, *Personal Memoirs,* vol. 1, 308.

p. 91, "I would rather . . ." Smith, *Grant,* 155.

p. 92, "Whichever party . . ." Maihafer, *The General and the Journalists,* 96.

p. 92-93, "No terms except . . ." Marshal-Cornwall, *Grant As Military Commander,* 61.

p. 93, "Buckner, you are . . ." Kendall D. Gott, *Where the South Lost the War: An Analysis of the Fort Henry–Fort Donelson Campaign, February 1862* (Mechanicsburg, PA: Stackpole Books, 2003), 262.

CHAPTER SIX: Lincoln's Man

p. 94, "Gen. Ulysses S. Grant . . ." Maihafer, *The General and the Journalists,* 98.

p. 96, "It is hard to . . ." Perret, *Ulysses S. Grant,* 178.

p. 96, "Do not hesitate . . ." Ibid., 179.

p. 97-98, "had no expectation . . ." Ulysses S. Grant, *The Civil War Memoirs of Ulysses S. Grant* (Edited by Brian M. Thomsen. New York: Tom Dougherty Associates, 2002),   81.

p. 98, "eyes and hopes . . ." Bruce Catton, *The American Heritage New History of the Civil War* (New York: Viking, 1996), 112.

p. 100, "Shall I make . . ." Smith, *Grant,* 200.

p. 100, "Retreat? No. I propose . . ." Ibid.

p. 101, "General, do you . . ." Leckie, *The Wars of America,* 421.

p. 101, "Shiloh was the . . ." Kaltman, *Cigars, Whiskey & Winning,* 79.

p. 103, "I can't spare . . ." Ibid., 80.

p. 103, "For myself I was . . ." Grant, *Civil War Memoirs,* 105.

p. 103, "I am satisfied . . ." Ibid., 107.

p. 104, "During the two . . ." Ibid., 115.

p. 105, "It looked to me . . ." Maihafer, *The General and the Journalists,* 132.

p. 105, "The fight began . . ." Marshal-Cornwall, *Grant As Military Commander,* 92.

p. 106, "I rather like . . ." Ibid., 109.

p. 109, "what rations of . . ." Benjamin F. Cooley III, "The Civil War, 1863," in *American Military History,* 239.

p. 111, "The heads of . . ." Ibid., 240.

p. 111-112, "I now determined . . ." Grant, *Civil War Memoirs,* 187.

p. 113, "The Father of Waters . . ." Stephen D. Engle, *The American Civil War: The War in the West 1861–July 1863* (Essential History series. Edited by Rebecca Cullen. Oxford, UK: Osprey Publishing, 2001), 65.

p. 113, "He doesn't worry . . ." Ibid.

CHAPTER SEVEN: The Way to Appomattox

p. 115, "the dead were . . ." Cooley, *American Military History,* 257.

p. 116, "acted like a duck . . ." Ibid., 258.

p. 116, "Sherman was to get . . ." Ulysses S. Grant, *Personal Memoirs of U. S. Grant,* Vol. 2 (Scituate, MA: Digital Scanning, 1998), 88.

p. 117, "the utter rout and . . ." Maihafer, *The General and the Journalists,* 180.

p. 117, "The siege of . . ." Ibid., 181.

p. 118, "My son, you will . . ." Ibid., 184.

p. 119, "headquarters [with] armies . . ." Richard J. Somers, "Grant, Ulysses Simpson," in *Encyclopedia of the American Civil War,* 868.

p. 119, "There were . . . seventeen . . ." Ibid.

p. 119, "My general plan . . ." Ibid.

p. 121, "Lee, with the capital . . ." Grant, *Personal Memoirs,* vol. 2, 146.

p. 121, "Lee's army will . . ." Maihafer, *The General and the Journalists,* 191.

p. 122, "You I propose to . . ." Grant, *Personal Memoirs,* vol. 2, 131.

p. 123, "I will agree to . . ." Kaltman, *Cigars, Whiskey & Winning,* 211.

p. 123, "Oh, I am heartily . . ." James McPherson, "Failed Southern Strategies" (in *MHQ: The Quarterly Journal of Military History,* Summer 1999, Volume II, Number 4), 67.

p. 124, "I have always . . ." Kaltman, *Cigars, Whiskey & Winning,* 225.

p. 125, "My own opinion . . ." Somers, *Encyclopedia of the American Civil War,* 869.

p. 128, "To his Excellency . . ." Maihafer, *The General and the Journalists,* 209.

p. 129, "the last rays of . . ." Chris E. Fonvielle, Jr., "Wilmington, North Carolina," in *Encyclopedia of the American Civil War,* 2121.

p. 130, "Sheridan reached . . ." Grant, *Civil War Memoirs,* 445, 446.

p. 132, "General: The results . . ." Russell F. Weigley, *A Great Civil War: A Military and Political History, 1861–1865* (Bloomington: Indiana University Press, 2000), 440.

p. 132, "Though not entertaining . . ." Ibid.

p. 132, "I have fought my . . ." Ibid.

p. 132-133, "I now request . . ." Ibid., 441.

p. 133, "General Lee was . . ." Grant, *Civil War Memoirs,* 473.

p. 133-135, "The arms, artillery . . ." Marshal-Cornwall, *Grant As Military Commander,* 220.

p. 135, "This will have . . ." Ibid.

p. 135, "There was no . . ." Lisa Lauterbach Laskin, "Appomattox Court House," in *Encyclopedia of the American Civil War,* 71.

p. 135, "[T]he first thing . . ." Smith, *Grant,* 93.

CHAPTER EIGHT: Chief Executive

p. 136, "all the armies . . ." Perret, *Ulysses S. Grant,* 361.

p. 137, "The President was . . ." Ibid., 362.

p. 137, "incontestably the greatest . . ." Smith, *Grant,* 412.

p. 138, "For some reason . . ." Ibid., 410.

p. 141, "Grant, Grant, Grant," Ibid., 427.

p. 141-142, "No man is authorized . . ." Ibid.

p. 142, "I have never been . . ." Ibid.

p. 142, "such an infernal liar," Ibid.

p. 143, "Let us have peace," Perret, *Ulysses S. Grant,* 379.

p. 143, "I am afraid . . ." Ibid., 380.

p. 144, "The election of . . ." Maihafer, *The General and the Journalists,* 227.

p. 144, "The responsibilities . . ." *Ulysses S. Grant Chronology,*
21.

p. 147, "The payment of this . . ." Smith, *Grant,* 480.

p. 147-148, "gold or its equivalent . . ." Ibid.

p. 148, "shall not be denied . . ." George Childs Kohn,
Dictionary of Historic Documents (Rev. ed. New York: Facts
On File, 2003), 153.

p. 149, "I urgently recommend . . ." Smith, *Grant,* 546.

p. 150, "citizens of every . . ." Ibid., 547.

p. 150, "arrest and break . . ." Ibid.

p. 150, "There has never . . ." Ibid.

p. 151-152, "I acknowledge . . ." *Ulysses S. Grant Chronology,*
23–24.

p. 153, "a departure from . . ." Smith, *Grant,* 579.

p. 154, "Let no guilty man escape," *Ulysses S. Grant Chronology,* 24.

p. 155, "the most scrupulously . . ." Perret, *Ulysses S. Grant,*
443.

p. 155, "I do not think . . ." Ibid.

p. 155-156, "It was my fortune . . ." *Ulysses S. Grant
Chronology,* 24–25.

p. 157, "I was never as . . ." Perret, *Ulysses S. Grant,* 446.

p. 157, "It is not believed . . ." Maihafer, *The General and the
Journalists,* 261.

p. 157, "Man proposes and . . ." Grant, *Personal Memoirs,* vol.
1, 7.

Bibliography

Catton, Bruce. *Grant Moves South.* Edison, NJ: Castle Books, 2000.

——————. *The American Heritage New History of the Civil War.* New York: Viking, 1996.

Commager, Henry Steele, ed. *The Civil War Archive: The History of the Civil War in Documents.* Revised and expanded by Erik Bruun. New York: Black Dog & Leventhal Publishers, 2000.

Conger, Arthur L. *The Rise of U. S. Grant.* New York: Da Capo Press, 1996.

Cowley, Robert, ed. *With My Face to the Enemy: Perspectives on the Civil War.* New York: G. P. Putnam's Sons, 2001.

Dupuy, Trevor N., Curt John, and David L. Bongard. *The Harper Encyclopedia of Military Biography.* New York: HarperCollins, 1992.

Ehrlich, Ev. *Grant Speaks.* New York: Warner Books, 2000.

Engle, Stephen D. *The American Civil War: The War in the West 1861–July 1863.* Essential History series. Edited by Rebecca Cullen. Oxford, UK: Osprey Publishing, 2001.

Gott, Kendall D. *Where the South Lost the War: An Analysis of the Fort Henry–Fort Donelson Campaign, February 1862.* Mechanicsburg, PA: Stackpole Books, 2003.

Grant, Ulysses S. *The Civil War Memoirs of Ulysses S. Grant.* Edited by Brian M. Thomsen. New York: Tom Dougherty Associates, 2002.

——————. *Personal Memoirs of U. S. Grant.* Vols. 1 and 2. Scituate, MA: Digital Scanning, 1998.

Heidler, David S., and Jeanne T. Heidler, eds. *Encyclopedia of the American Civil War: A Political, Social, and Military History.* New York: W. W. Norton, 2000.

Kaltman, Al. *Cigars, Whiskey & Winning Leadership Lessons from General Ulysses S. Grant.* Paramus, NJ: Prentice Hall Press, 1998.

Katcher, Philip, and Tony Bryan. *American Civil War Artillery 1861–1865, Field and Heavy Artillery.* Botley, Oxford, UK: Osprey, 2001.

Kohn, George Childs. *Dictionary of Historic Documents.* Rev. ed. New York: Facts On File, 2003.

Leckie, Robert. *The Wars of America.* Vol. I. Updated Edition. New York: HarperCollins, 1993.

Lyman, Theodore. *With Grant and Meade from the Wilderness to Appomattox.* Lincoln: University of Nebraska Press, 1994.

Maihafer, Harry J. *The General and the Journalists: Ulysses S. Grant, Horace Greeley, and Charles Dana.* Washington, DC: Brassey's, 2001.

Marshal-Cornwall, James. *Grant As Military Commander.* New York: Barnes & Noble, 1995.

Matloff, Maurice, ed. *American Military History.* Vol. 1: 1775–1902. Conshohocken, PA: Combined Books, 1996.

Patterson, Gerard A. *Rebels from West Point.* Mechanicsburg, PA: Stackpole Books, 2002.

Perret, Geoffrey. *Ulysses S. Grant: Soldier & President.* New York: Modern Library, 1999.

Rhea, Gordon C. *Cold Harbor: Grant and Lee, May 26–June 3, 1864.* Baton Rouge: Louisiana State University Press, 2002.

Smith, Jean Edward. *Grant.* New York: Simon & Schuster, 2001.

Weigley, Russell F. *A Great Civil War: A Military and Political History, 1861–1865.* Bloomington: Indiana University Press, 2000.

Web sites

http://www.mscomm.com/~ulysses/page11.html
Interview with Hannah Simpson Grant.

http://www.lib.siu.edu/projects/usgrant/grant2.htm
Ulysses S. Grant chronology.

http://www.saints.css.edu/mkelsey/hors1.html
Ulysses S. Grant and his horses.

http://www.whitehouse.gov/history/presidents/ug18.html
The White House official biography of U. S. Grant, the eighteenth president.

http://www.lib.siu.edu/projects/usgrant/
The online home of the Ulysses S. Grant Association, hosted by Southern Illinois University.

http://www.nps.gov/ulsg/
A Web site by the National Park Service for White Haven, Grant's one-time home.

http://www.pbs.org/wgbh/amex/grant/
Information and excerpts from the PBS film about Ulysses S. Grant.

Index

Porter, David D., 108-109, *137*
Price, Sterling, 105-106

Resaca de la Palma, battle of, 42-44, *42*
Ringgold, Major, 41, *41*
Rosecrans, William S., 19, *105*, 105-106, 114, 116

Santa Anna, Antonio López de, 47, 50, 53-55
Scott, Winfield, 21-22, *22*, 26, *47*, 49-56, *53*, 58, 85-86
Scott, Sir Walter, 21
Second Seminole War, 36
Sheridan, Philip, 121-122, 127-131, *128*
Sherman, William Tecumseh, 18, 83, 94, 97, 109-111, 114, 117, 122, 125, 127-129, *128*, 137
Shiloh, battle of, 99-103, *99*, *101*, 118, *134*
Smith, Charles F., 90, 92, 96
Specie Resumption Act, 154
Spotsylvania, battle of, 124
Stanton, Edwin McMasters, 116

Taylor, Zachary, 33-37, *35*, 38-45, *40*, 48-50, 78-79, 133
Terry, Alfred H., 129
Thomas, George H., 19, 36, 115-116, *128*, 128
Thomas, Lorenzo, 79
Thorton, Seth, 38
Tilghman, Lloyd, 88
Tyler, John, 33-34

United States Military Academy, 9, 16-24, *17*, 36, 50, 58, 69, 74, 78, 84-85, 92, 96, *134*

Van Dorn, Earl, 19, 36, 102, 106
Veracruz, battle of, 49-52, *51*
Vicksburg, battle of, 106-113, *107*, *108*, *111*, 114, 118, 124-145, *134*

War of 1812, 10, 36
Washburne, Elihu, 78, 143
Whiskey Ring scandal, 154-155
Wilderness, battle of the, 123
Worth, William J., 45, 56

Yates, Richard, 78, 80, 81-82
Young, John Russell, 155, 157

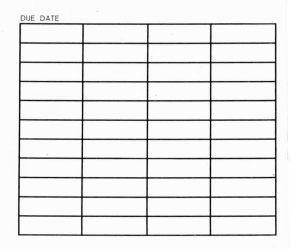

JUV
973.82
GRANT   Rice, Earle

              Ulysses S. Grant

DUE DATE
